PRAYERS FROM
Riverside

UPDATED

PRAYERS FROM

Riverside

UPDATED

Leo S. Thorne, editor

THE
PILGRIM
PRESS
Cleveland

The Pilgrim Press, 700 Prospect Avenue, Cleveland, Ohio 44115
thepilgrimpress.com

Library of Congress Cataloging-in-Publication Data
Prayers from Riverside
    Prayers from Riverside updated / edited by Leo S. Thorne ;
    foreword by Stephen H. Phelps.
        pages   cm
    Previously published as: Prayers from Riverside. 1983.
    ISBN 978-0-8298-1934-2 (alk. paper)
    1. Prayers. 2. Prayer – Christianity – Sermons. 3. Sermons,
American. I. Thorne, Leo S., 1944 – II. Riverside Church
(New York, N.Y.) III. Title.
BV245.P852 2012
242'.3 – dc23   2012033085

Contents

Foreword
by Stephen H. Phelps
vii

Revised Introduction
by Leo S. Thorne
1

Six Ways in Which
Modern People Can Pray
by Harry Emerson Fosdick

5

PRAYERS FROM RIVERSIDE

Foreword

Even when its covers are closed, the prayers in a volume of prayers keep praying. The eye lingering on the slim binding renews the blessing. It is as if all who are assembled within stand at the door with a holy greeting. You have only to open the passageway again.

Many who read in these pages will hear the timbre of the voices of the pastors who prayed them. Some may remember the very morning a petition was offered. Most all will recall the great arched nave of Riverside, where these words flew down for their Master to heal and to guide, to challenge and to comfort and to give thanks. May a fragrance of that awe and peace and restless hope from which Sabbath is breathed bedew you.

Here are assembled the reverend brothers and sisters who prayed Riverside through—in courage, in sorrow, in edgeless faith, in every generation since its dedication. I pray that this indissoluble reunion of the shepherds of the church may stand as a watch on your shelf for the hope you cannot live without, that God works love into the clay of what's human and, by grace, love is all you touch, no matter how it seemed. Love abides.

Rev. Stephen H. Phelps
Interim Senior Minister
The Riverside Church
December 2011

Revised Introduction

"Prayer is a tremendous spiritual force," Dr. Harry Emerson Fosdick once declared. And it is my hope that all who read through the pages of this volume will take a cue from that affirmation and find great spiritual upliftment in the prayers presented here. It was no easy task to select a certain number of prayers from all the stirring prayers that have been uttered at The Riverside Church in New York City, especially since variety and virtuosity complicated the intention. Yet the exercise was profoundly moving and delightful. My experience with the project was especially meaningful, and the challenge only reinforced the thought that if these prayers are taken seriously—and they should be—they can be a sustaining source of spiritual strength.

One cannot come in contact with The Riverside Church without quickly discovering its staunch mission and philosophy. This interdenominational, interracial, international church espouses a social interpretation of the gospel that affirms that the message of Jesus Christ is vitally concerned with all aspects of life, whether they be spiritual, moral, political, economic, or cultural. This message has often been reiterated in the several prayers of the ministers. This book presents some of these prayers in the hope that they will help both those who want to escape the busyness of the everyday world and those who want to prepare for public prayer. The selections also attempt to follow the liturgical sequence, not only because it seemed to make meaningful order out of the wealth of prayers available, but also because the rhythm fits comfortably with the scope of Riverside's concern for the needs of individuals and for the pressing issues of society at large. The book begins with a particularly helpful sermon, "Six Ways in Which Modern [People] Can Pray," by Harry Emerson Fosdick, and ends with "A City-Dweller's Prayer," an ironically universal prayer by Ernest T. Campbell.

Two unique features of this book merit special attention. First, the prayers offer a variety of styles and moods, rendering the selections suitable for almost any occasion and satisfying to different tastes. Second, the language of the prayers—the lofty Elizabethan with its lyrical cadences and the modern with its spontaneous rhythm—reflects the special and distinct personalities of the ministers, making the selections both refreshing and harmoniously diverse. On the one hand, we can find Dr. Fosdick stirring up the heavenly hosts with statements like "Eternal Spirit, from whom all things come and in whom all things consist, grant us, who are spirits, that we may worship thee." On the other hand, we can find William Sloane Coffin Jr. praying with no less ardor for the "fun of St. Valentine's Day" and the "lonely road that leads to peace." These facets make the book reflect the rich diversity of the Riverside parish and place the reader in the thick of this richness.

We focused primarily on the pastoral prayers of the senior ministers over the years: Harry Emerson Fosdick, 1930–1946; Robert J. McCracken, 1946–1967; Ernest T. Campbell, 1968–1976; William Sloane Coffin Jr., 1977–1987; Eugene E. Laubach, 1961–1991; and George Thomas, 1977–1986.

The revised edition includes a foreword by Stephen H. Phelps, Interim Senior Minister. Two senior ministers who served Riverside after the first edition of the book was released, James Forbes Jr., who served from 1989 to 2007 and Brad Braxton, who served in 2008–2009, have prayers in this revised book. Two women clergy, Fanny Erickson, 1991–2006 and Joan

Kavanaugh, 1981–2011 are also represented in this new text. On request, the editor has added four of his pastoral prayers given while he served on the volunteer staff during Dr. Coffin's tenure as senior minister.

Finally, we agree that the book would be incomplete without a section of those poignant Riverside prayers of confession, for which we thank all whose selections were used.

This original project could not have been completed without the dedicated assistance of a number of special people. First mentioned must be Judith Stein, the associate editor. Judy brought valuable professional skill and careful comments and insights that helped shape the evolution of the book. I am also particularly grateful to Linda Van Haste for her assistance in developing the idea for the book and for her aid in selecting the prayers of confession. I received invaluable help from not a few Riversiders, who assisted either in selecting specific prayers from the enormous number with which we had to work or who provided some measure of unfailing service. These people include Jean Andralliski, Barbara Brianzeva, Ann Cleaves, Sarah Cunningham, Emily Deeter, Carolyn Morehead, Cheryl Parham, Gena Phoenix, and Ruth Watson. Yet I end where I should have begun, with sincere gratitude to the families of the ministers and to the many members and friends of Riverside who supported the project. In this revised edition, Diane Vescovi and Yvonne Martinez Thorne provided significant assistance.

Editor's note: Although we were mindful not to take great liberties with the ministers' prayers, we agreed that inclusive language would be more appropriate to the prayers today. What is striking, however, is that Dr. Fosdick particularly seemed to be ahead of his time, even though he did not have the benefit of today's thinking. In many of his prayers, he used current expressions such as "humankind."

Six Ways in Which
Modern People Can Pray

Harry Emerson Fosdick

One wishes one could speak about prayer without using the word. If one could approach a subject like this freshly, could outflank the preconceived ideas of it and surprise people into the discovery of prayer's reality before they even guessed that one was talking about prayer, that would be ideal. For words like "prayer" have a long history. They come to us encrusted with old practices in which no intelligent person can indulge. Today I am asking you not to blockade the road of this sermon with preconceived opinions. At least give us a fair chance to talk together about some of the real experiences of prayer.

To many people, for example, prayer suggests begging the cosmic God to run errands for us, and that seems to them absurd. Of course it is absurd. But why shut ourselves off from the rich and rewarding experiences of real prayer by preconceived opinions picked up in childhood, it may be, or heard of, heaven knows where?

Indeed, let us start with a word of Jesus which in the first instance had nothing to do with prayer. In the parable of the sower, Jesus said of the seeds falling on thin soil among rocky places that "they had not much earth: and straightway they sprang up, because they had no deepness of earth: and when the sun was risen, they were scorched; and because they had no root, they withered away." So! Because they had no root—there is a text on prayer.

Here, then, are six kinds of prayer which bring to life deepness of earth and strong rootage in it—all of them possible to an intelligent modern person who believes in God at all, and in this difficult time especially and desperately needed.

First, the prayer of interior relaxation and serenity. It is a prayer which does not beg God for anything but rests the soul back. To be sure, if someone is to rest back successfully, that person must have something deep to rest back upon, as though to say, "The eternal God is thy refuge, and underneath are the everlasting arms." Even in its simplest form prayer does involve great matters. John Tyndall, the nineteenth-century scientist, although an outspoken agnostic, said this: "Often unreasonable, if not contemptible, in its purer forms, prayer hints at disciplines which few of us can neglect without moral loss." So! Even an agnostic may have interior disciplines akin to prayer. But happy is the one who, when facing the inevitable necessity of resting back, has something deep within to rest back upon!

Now, the God of the New Testament peculiarly meets this need. For where is the God of the New Testament? Granted that, as in the Old Testament, God still is The Eternal, holding Orion and the Pleiades in leash, from everlasting to everlasting the Creator—yet where especially is God's dwelling as the New Testament pictures it, the place where we meet God, where our experience of God is consummated and fulfilled? Listen: "Know ye not that ye are a temple of God, and that the Spirit of God dwelleth in you?" "Behold, I stand at the door and knock: if any man hear my voice and open the door, I will come in to him, and will sup with him, and he with me." "God is love; and he that abideth in love abideth in God, and God abideth in him." Praying to such a God is not vainly reaching outside oneself to a distant deity, not exploding oneself, as it were, toward high heaven in a wild endeavor to catch the cosmic ear. Prayer to God, in its simplest form, is resting back upon a divine presence personally possessed and intimately known. How do people live without that experience?

There are two aspects to every strong life—fruitage and rootage, activity and receptivity, tension and relaxation, working hard and resting back. When first we named this kind of prayer, did some young ardent spirit here feel scornful of it? So did you say, prayer is letting go, lying down, taking it easy, resting back, going to sleep? To which I answer: Do you really feel scornful about rest and sleep? Have you ever had insomnia, when you could not sleep, been so tense that you could not relax, so harried you could not let go? Those who cannot rest cannot work; those who cannot let go cannot hang on; those who lose serenity within have lost everything without. My consultation hours fill up with men and women who have mastered the techniques of activity and aggressiveness and whose lives are going all to pieces because they have mastered no other techniques at all.

Listen, then, to this prayer from the great tradition of the church: "Let my soul take refuge from the crowding turmoil of worldly thoughts beneath the shadow of thy wings; let my heart, this sea of restless waves, find peace in thee, O God." Who said that? Saint Augustine. A weak man? One of the most tremendous characters in history, from his early struggles with himself until at last, bishop of Hippo in North Africa, he fell on sleep while the invading barbarians were hammering at the city gates and the Roman Empire was falling around his ears. He never could have stood up as he did throughout such a tumultuous life without that kind of prayer. That man had roots.

In the second place, the prayer of affirmation. This prayer also does not beg God for anything but goes up before the face of God and there remembers and affirms the great convictions which blow trumpets in the soul and rouse its powers to action. "The Lord is my shepherd; I shall not want"—that is prayer. "Our Father who art in heaven, Hallowed be thy name"—that is prayer. "I thank my God upon every remembrance of you"—that is prayer. "Therefore will not we fear, though the earth be removed, and though the mountains be carried into the midst of the sea; though the waters thereof roar and be troubled, though the mountains shake with the swelling thereof. . . . The Lord of hosts is with us; the God of Jacob is our refuge"—that is prayer. It is not begging; it is affirming, putting at the center of one's mind those great convictions of faith which enlarge and elevate, empower, and dignify the soul.

One of the most moving sermons of our generation was preached in Aberdeen by Dr. Arthur John Gossip, a powerful Scottish minister. His wife had died without warning, and one of the loveliest of homes had been broken up with terrific suddenness. Taking for the subject of his next sermon "But When Life Tumbles In, What Then?" he made an affirmation of faith which shook Aberdeen and which even in cold print cannot be read now and soon forgotten. Of course that man prayed, but evidently it was the kind of praying which held at the center of his thought not so much his trouble as his faith, which threw around and over and underneath his trouble great convictions, as though, like the psalmist, he too were saying to God, "Though I walk through the valley of the shadow of death, I will fear no evil; for thou art with me; thy rod and thy staff, they comfort me." And so powerful is such affirmatory prayer that he could end his sermon to his people by quoting Hopeful from *The Pilgrim's Progress*, halfway through the last dark river, calling back to his friend, "Be of good cheer, my brother, for I feel the bottom, and it is sound."

Indeed, so influential is this affirmatory process that it makes praying dangerous. I mean that some people pray about trouble in such a way that, putting trouble in the center of attention, they come out more troubled than they were before. Some people pray about sexual temptation in such wise that, putting that in the center of their thought and keeping it there, though they are talking to God about it, they end worse than they began. Some people pray about discouragement so that they emerge more discouraged than they started, because their prayer has only served to concentrate their attention the more on their disheartenment. You will find no praying like that in scripture. Paul was in trouble, in prison, facing death. Listen to him pray: "I bow my knees unto the Father, from whom every family in heaven and on earth is named, that he would grant you, according to the riches of his glory, that ye may be strengthened with power through his Spirit in the inward man; that Christ may dwell in your hearts through faith; to the end that ye, being rooted and grounded in love, may be strong to apprehend with all the saints what is the breadth and length and height and depth, and to know the love of Christ which passeth knowledge, that ye may be filled unto all the fullness of God." That is affirmatory prayer. How do people live without it?

An old legend says that after the angels had rebelled in heaven and had been cast out into their eternal prison, they were asked what they missed most and they answered, "The sound of the trumpets in the morning." Aye, that is prayer.

In the third place, the prayer of spiritual companionship. This prayer also does not beg God for anything but habitually enters into inward fellowship with God. It is the prayer that says with Jesus, "I am not alone, because God is with me." Who can properly estimate the control over our lives conferred on us by the fact that we can choose our interior spiritual companionships? Many things in the outer world we cannot choose; there

necessity often decides not only the circumstances which
shall befall us but even the company which we must keep. But
within ourselves we can choose our company. There no hand
can shut the door against a visitor whom we would entertain.
There we are masters of our hospitality. There we can maintain
a habitual spiritual fellowship.

Someone here may be saying, this is a modernist's idea
of prayer and not at all the old conception on which the his-
toric church has been nourished. To which I answer, Who was
it said that if a person uses words, that is not prayer; that if a
person uses ordered thoughts, that is not prayer; that only
when one goes deeper than words and ordered thoughts can
go and is wrapped in the sense of a spiritual companionship
is one praying? Who said that? Savonarola. Who was it said
that prayer is establishing "ourselves in a sense of God's presence by continually conversing with God"? Brother Lawrence,
a medieval Catholic saint. Who was it said that prayer meant
to him making "frequent colloquies or short discoursings
between God and his own soul"? Jeremy Taylor, an old Prot-
estant leader. Friends, to the great souls of the church prayer
has meant the maintenance of a habitual spiritual fellowship.

Here the limelight falls upon one of the most important
things that can be said about prayer: Its worst perversions,
superstitions, and caricatures are associated with the idea
of it as an emergency measure. People get into a tight place
and then try to pray themselves out of it. As the psalmist
says, "They . . . are at their wits' end. Then they cry unto God
in their trouble." That is a third-rate way of praying—trying
to use God, as the old Greek dramatists used Zeus, a deus
ex machina swung over the stage to unravel the plot when it
was so tangled that human wit could not unravel it. Who so
thinks of prayer has made magic of it and at the last will discover that the great God is too august to be a suddenly called

errand boy running to answer our frantically pushed buttons. The worst perversions of prayer come from treating it thus as an emergency measure. That is not the way we treat friendship. The glory of a friend is dependable fellowship. The glory of the Unseen Friend is habitual companionship. Then when an emergency comes one goes, like Jesus to the Garden, traveling an accustomed path to a familiar presence for a brief colloquy, to emerge again to face the wrath of devils and the scorn of human beings. Souls who pray this way have roots.

In the fourth place, the prayer of moral conflict. The most decisive battles of the world are fought not on external battlefields but in the consciences of human beings. The destiny of Israel's nation was in the wilderness with Moses alone beside the burning bush. The destiny of humankind was with Jesus in the desert alone with his temptation. The hope of the church was on the Damascus Road with Paul "not disobedient unto the heavenly vision." One stands in awe before these inner battlefields. What thus is true in the large, in the small is true of each of us: Our major conflicts are within.

Praying means carrying these conflicts up before the face of God and fighting them out in the light of the Highest before we have to fight them out in the world. Underline this: No one can extemporize character. Our great decisions have to be made triumphantly within before they can be made triumphantly without. Alas for the one who does not know that inner place of prayer where the great decisions can be made!

Consider this autobiographical reminiscence from Robert Louis Stevenson. "Go," he says, "the first grey, east-windy day into the Caledonian Station, if it looks at all as it did of yore: I met Satan there." One wonders what it was he met there. All unsuspectingly young Stevenson passed into the Caledonian Station, but years afterward he was still remembering the terrific impact of that shock—he met Satan there. So in every realm life does ambush us. We must be ready beforehand. It is too late to get ready after the ambush has been sprung. No one can extemporize character. We need an inner place where the decisions are made first.

As you see, I am talking not so much about the theory as about the experience of prayer. All through life run vital functions whose theories keep changing but whose experience persists. Agriculture, for example. How changing and varied have been the theories of agriculture this last quarter of a century! But agriculture persists; we must go on growing things to eat, no matter how the theories shift. So prayer's explanations alter, but its experiences persist. We, like our forebears, must have a high and inward place where we fight out our major conflicts in the presence of God before we have to fight them out in the world.

No one, I think, ever described this function of prayer so vividly as did Chinese Gordon. He had temptations so terrific one wonders that he ever came through. He whimsically named one of them Agag after the Amalekite king in the Old Testament. Listen to him then in a letter to his sister: "My constant prayer is against Agag, who, of course, is here, and as insinuating as ever," and again, "One feels inclined to withdraw from the combat altogether, and go into seclusion; but even there I expect Agag would pursue in some form." Says one biographer, "He wrestled with 'Agag'" and George Adam Smith reports that more than once he said, "I had a hard half hour this morning hewing Agag in pieces before the Lord." I commend to you this indispensable experience—"hewing Agag in pieces before the Lord."

In the fifth place, the prayer of strong desire. As some of you have been correctly thinking, prayer is more than resting back, or affirming faith before the face of God, or seeking an interior companionship, or carrying our conflicts up into the light of the Highest. Prayer is strong desire. It comes out of our deep needs, and it cries for the things we want.

Were I to ask you about the condition of your "prayer life," that might sound to you like a pious question and, half-sheepishly, you might try to tell me that you have very little of it. But if I should ask you about your life of desire, you could not tell me that you have very little of that. That is the heart of you—your strong and clamorous desire. Well, let us not fool ourselves with the conventionality of language. Desire is prayer. Beneath all the things we commonly call praying, what we do verily want of life is our genuine prayer. We never know anyone, then, until we know his or her desire. We know Admiral Robert Peary when we hear him say, "The determination to reach the Pole had become so much a part of my being that, strange as it may seem, I long ago ceased to think of myself save as an instrument for the attainment of that end." We know John Knox when we hear him pray, "Give me Scotland, or I die!"

Have you ever read the Beatitudes of Jesus and been astonished that prayer is not mentioned? Strange, isn't it, that this master of prayer, to whom it meant so much, should speak these great beatitudes of the spiritual life and leave prayer out! But we are mistaken. Prayer is there, not in word but, deeper, in reality. "Blessed are they that hunger and thirst after righteousness: for they shall be filled." That is prayer, life's hunger and thirst.

So prayer is a tremendous force. Controlling desire can roll down through the center of a person's life like the Mississippi, which, flowing through the center of the continent, calls in tributary streams from every side until, a flood, it pours out into the Gulf of Mexico.

Now, because desire is one's real prayer, praying is dangerous. We commonly hear folks complain because their prayers are not answered, but I say, Alas, look around you and see the people on every side ruined because their real prayers have been answered! Underneath the formal supplications which we offer when we put on court clothes and come up to the sanctuary piously to ask what it seems meet to ask—beneath such formal praying, our veritable demands on life, the cravings around which our lives are organized, inevitably tend to be answered. Indeed, we use a slang phrase when some bitter rebuff or unkindly consequence falls upon someone. He asked for that, we say. Just so! Of how much of our trouble is that true—we asked for that!

Go through this congregation now, and our major problems concern our desires, their conflicts, their perversity, their waywardness, their power, so hard to handle. Ah, my soul, carry up your life of desire before the face of the Most High, there to be unified, organized, elevated, purified, directed to great ends, saying as Jesus did in the Garden, "Not my will, but thine, be done." How can anyone live well without some such process in his or her soul?

In the sixth place, the prayer of released power. One never ceases to be astonished at the number of people who think that prayer means getting God to do what they want done. But the very saying of that ought to prove its fallacy. God, at my beck and call to do what I want done because I want it—the perspective is all wrong in that, as though the mountain must come to Muhammad and not Muhammad to the mountain. No! Prayer is not a way of getting God to do what we want but a way of putting ourselves in such relationship with God that God can do in and for and through us what God wants. Prayer is not a magic means by which we control God but a humble means by which God can control us, find gang way through us, release divine power and purpose in us.

Did you ever try to teach music to a child who did not want to learn music? That is a baffling task. Here is the whole world of music, and you, more than willing to give a creative share in it to the child, are baffled, frustrated, and stopped for this so simple reason: There is no prayer for music in the child. So at last, like a great reservoir waiting in vain for an outlet, the world of music finds in that child no release and through him or her no revelation. See! Without prayer there are some things God cannot say to us, for prayer is the listening ear. Without prayer there are some things God cannot give to us, for prayer is the hospitable heart. Without prayer there are some things God cannot do through us, for prayer is the cooperative will.

Therefore, I beg of you not to say that I presented prayer merely as a subjective experience without objective consequences. Friends, the most tremendous objective consequences on earth come from released power. Even in the physical world we do not by our sciences create power; we release it, with world-transforming consequence. So, when David Livingstone prayed about Africa, "May God in mercy permit me to do something for the cause of Christ in these dark places of the earth!" he did not change God's intention, but he did change God's action. He did not alter God's purpose, but he did release it. There was a fresh invasion of the world by God through Livingstone. Who can set limits to the possibilities of that?

Six kinds of prayer that give us deepness of earth and strong rootage in it! Not one of them, I think, is shut out from any intelligent person if he or she believes in God at all. Friends, we miss such praying, not because of the keenness of our intellect, but because of the shallowness of our lives.

Prayer

Eternal God, we lift up the prayer that the disciples long ago presented to Jesus: Lord, teach us how to pray. In the spirit of Christ. Amen.

PRAYERS FROM *Riverside*

Advent

O God, with the turning of the year we begin our pilgrimage toward Christmas and the child who grew to be our king. We come like shepherds, lonely and seeking. We come like Wise Men, looking in the wrong places for God's gifts. We come because year after year we have heard the angels sing and been reminded of the gift of love. Help us, in these days of Advent, to prepare ourselves, so that when the star shines over a stable and the angels sing the good news, we may be ready to receive it because our hearts are open and our spirits are receptive to your leading.

O mighty God, you made our world and us and all things to serve you. Now make our world ready for your rule. We thank you for the promises of peace and healing and justice. We pray for a time when violence and crying shall end and all your children shall live in peace, honoring one another in justice and love. Go before us, O God, drawing us into the future you have prepared for us. In the name of Christ we pray.

Amen.   —*Eugene E. Laubach*

God, that we are alive,
 that food is delicious to the taste,
 that the ground is firm beneath our tread,
 that rest can compensate for toil,
 that earth might be fair and all her children blest,
thy name be praised.

We thank thee for friends who care,
    for ways that open when every door seems shut,
    for the reality of forgiveness—human and divine,
    for major purposes that make life's minor irritations
        bearable,
    for the confidence that our gravest ills will yield to sacrifice
        and toil.
We thank thee for thyself—ground and source of every good—
and especially for thy love, that no resistance can diminish
and no need exhaust.

With all thy people in every corner of creation, we count it joy
to praise thy name.

Through Jesus Christ our Lord.

We pray today for those who are up against hard numbers:
    those in prison who serve a fixed sentence;
    those in the hospital whose life expectancy is a matter of
        days;
    those who must make a payment on a note at a set time;
    those being forced to move to unfamiliar quarters, on a
        date already assigned;
    those who must retire from the only life they know on a day
        already circled;
    those who know that their income from work or welfare
        cannot meet their family needs;
    those who find a deadline staring them in the face as they
        agonize over a decision.

O thou who art the Source of life, make us sensitive to those
who feel such pressures, knowing that it is a matter of grace
and not of merit that we are not there ourselves. And make our
extremity thine opportunity to save.

Through Jesus Christ our Lord.

We dare now to pray for ourselves, ashamed that we have done so little with so much, yet struggling to offer thee a more obedient service.

> Give us keener self-understanding—as keen as we can bear at one sitting—lest we think of ourselves more highly, or lowly, than we ought.
>
> Give us a sense of what is vital in life—lest we squander our years and waste our attention on inflated trifles.
>
> Give us a due regard for our unity with all people, lest we think in tribal patterns and forget that thou art Ruler of all the earth.

We ask, God, for ourselves the most meaningful Advent season we have ever known.

> Drive us to our knees;
>> to the Book;
>> to an awareness of our sin;
>> to a careful searching of our virtues;
>> to a serious examination of words and terms so glibly sung and spoken.

Measure us, O God, according to thy judgments, but take not thy mercy from us.

> And grant that when Christmas morning breaks for us this year, we may have something more to show for our much running about than tired feet, wrapped presents, and regrets for cards not sent.
>
> When thou saidst, "Seek ye my face," my heart said unto thee, "Thy face, God, will I seek."

Through Jesus Christ our Lord. Amen.

—Ernest T. Campbell

O God, who art our light and our salvation, enable us to enter into and abide in the secret place of the Most High, and may the shadow of the almighty be our covering defense. Bring us close to the things that are infinite and eternal. Grant us grace to behold the heavenly vision, that in the strength of it we may do the work of life without haste and without weariness.

With gratitude we make mention of the blessings which thou dost bountifully bestow upon us. We thank thee for this day of rest and gladness and ask that we may learn to use it for thy glory, for the enrichment of our lives and in the service of others. We thank thee for this sanctuary; its beauty feeds our souls, its quiet searches and solemnizes our hearts, its associations revive memories of some whom we have loved long since and lost awhile. We thank thee for liberty of worship, freedom of assembly, an open Bible, and, remembering how dearly they were bought, we beseech thee to forgive us that we have prized them so little. Most of all we thank thee for Christ—Companion of the brave, Comforter of the sad, Refuge of the tempted, Friend of the fallen. Teach us to understand what was meant of old when he was called the power of God unto salvation, for our world stands in need of salvation—from fear, from despair, from malice. And we too need salvation. We have learned that we cannot save ourselves. Do for us what we cannot do. Help us to conquer hopeless brooding and faithless reflection. Fill us with a more complete trust in thee and stir up within us a desire for a more wholehearted surrender to thy will.

Make us to be at peace with all humankind, gracious in temper, generous in judgment, kind in word and in deed, quick to sense and to understand the needs and feelings of others. In our home life make us loving to one another, tender-hearted and considerate. Lift before us now a picture of what we should be and what we should do, and keep it before us when we take up again our daily tasks.

We pray for this nation and for all who are entrusted with the administration of its affairs. Take away from us the spirit of class war and prejudice. Let the disputes and differences that have arisen among us have a speedy and fair settlement, and may justice be established among us.

We pray for this church and for all the churches, that we may have strength for our tasks, wisdom for our responsibilities, and a message adequate to the demands of the hour. We pray for any of our number who have met with affliction or who have come face-to-face with a great sorrow; for those who are passing through the fires, that they may not be burned; for those who are in deep waters, that they may not be swept down; for those who are inwardly tormented, that thy life may flow into theirs with healing and tranquilizing power.

Through Jesus Christ our Lord. Amen.

—*Robert J. McCracken*

O God of all good gifts and wonderful surprises, this Advent season reminds us again of your continuing commitment to share your best with us. Nothing we have remotely compares to the gift of your Precious Son, whom we treasure in our lives beyond Christmas. And as the trees, lights, and presents, and the happy, festive smiles, even from strangers, all tell that Christmas is a-coming, may we who are your children indeed not be dazzled by the glitz of this season, but may we keep in mind that your King of Glory entered into human history to make us all like you, you who are the source and sustainer of all life.

We come to thank you for the joys and tears of the past week, and even for those things for which our hearts stubbornly refuse to be thankful, knowing only the limited present moment. We thank you for the Summit with our president and leaders of countries long separated by ancient grudges. They made a small but wise step along the long road to peace. May the momentum sparked by this possibility guide these men to be lavish with their imagination, to dream the reality of a world free from nuclear weapons. For the wages of the opposite will not be an ungodly nuclear war, but the continuing of all assortments of injustice and moral decay.

We thank you for the events of Friday night, which gave us an opportunity to begin to cope with Bill's leaving. As he goes off to Washington, may we at Riverside ever remember the words he so often prayed in this hallowed place, that you, our God, would "strengthen our resolve to see fulfilled, in the world around and in our time, all hopes for justice so long deferred, and keep us on the stony, long, and lonely road that leads to peace. May we think for peace, struggle for peace, and suffer for peace."

We come to also thank you for our restless lives, dear God, so often burdened, so complex at times, so lost, so baffled and so encumbered by the little stuff, which we make to be so much big stuff. Do you sometimes break out in holy laughter as you see us fussing around, thinking ourselves so important and having an exclusive on what is right and what is wrong; for taking ourselves so seriously and for tangling up, by our own little selves, the beautiful lives that you have given us? Remind us, Divine Spirit, that we see through a glass darkly; only you have the big picture, the whole picture. You ask us to dare to believe that you are doing what is best for our lives, but only as we yield them to you.

And, most righteous God, as much as we need you, we need one another. Let us work, love, play, and strive together for the things that really matter in this life, and thrive together with excellence, knowing that one day, face-to-face, we shall know as we are known. Let it never be said of us, in this holy season, that we missed our opportunity to give more than to receive; to feed the hungry more than to prepare festive meals for ourselves and our families; to visit the sick and homeless more than to visit with our friends and loved ones; and to heal old wounds and forgive more than to cherish negative, diminishing feelings.

What we ask for ourselves, in this season of Advent, Wonderful Creator, we ask for all people everywhere who are working to make our world what you intended it to be. These prayers we make in the name of the baby Jesus, our savior and friend. Amen.
                                                            —*Leo S. Thorne*

O God, whom we trust but do not fully understand; whom we love, but surely not with all our hearts, give us, we pray thee, not the kind of Christmas we want, but the kind we need.
    We live with a sense of crowdedness;
        remind us of the providence that marks a sparrow's fall.
    We live with a shrinking sense of personal worth;
        remind us of a love to which each soul is precious.
    We live with a sense of the years going by too quickly;
        remind us of abiding purposes in which all that comes
        to pass partakes of the eternal.
    We live with a sense of wrongs committed and good
            undone or unattempted;
        remind us that for such the shepherd seeks,
        our God waits.
Our souls take their rest, O God, in the joy of what thou art.
Let it be enough that thou art for us, with us, and within us.

Through Jesus Christ our Lord.

O thou who didst send thy Son among us that the Word might be made flesh, bless with thy favor and encouragement those in our time who would "flesh out" the scriptures and make credible the gospel to an unbelieving age:

> all who earnestly work for peace;
>
> all who deliberately live on less than they might in order to share with those who have less than they need;
>
> all who make it their business to plead the cause of the orphan, the prisoner, and the oppressed;
>
> all who stand up in any company to challenge racial slurs and expose prejudice;
>
> all who have trained themselves to listen with genuine concern to those who need an outlet for their grievances and cares;
>
> all who have gone to the trouble of learning the gospel well enough to be able to share it with others.

O thou who hast told us clearly in the drama of Bethlehem that words alone won't do, help us productively to couple what we say with what we are and do, lest our rhetoric outrun our deeds.

Through Jesus Christ our Lord.

O thou who hast chosen the weak things of earth to confound the mighty:

> Give us, thy people, so susceptible to size, so easily impressed by worldly rank and scope; give us, O God, an eye for mangers tucked away in stables and an ear for truth whose only fanfare is the rippled intuitions of the heart.
>
> Visit our sick with quiet assurance of thy care.
>
> Encircle the bereaved with thy warming, healing presence.
>
> Point out markers on the trail for those who have lost their way.

And douse with the cold waters of common sense any who
might this very day be on the verge of some destructive
action or decision.

The race is short, O God, even at its longest, and we would run
it well, and to thy glory.

Through Jesus Christ our Lord. Amen.   *—Ernest T. Campbell*

Christmastide

O God, our Father/Mother, we thank thee for Christmas: for gifts given and gifts received; for family gatherings in which those separated gather together for a time; for letters and cards from those from whom we have not heard for long, we give thee thanks, O God. For the spirit of good will which is all through the land; for this time when people remember if only for a little while that it is more blessed to give than to receive; for this time when people find happiness in bringing happiness to others, we give thee thanks, O God.

O God our Mother, bless those for whom there is little joy at Christmastime. Bless those who are aged and alone and who have no one left to remember them. Bless those who have lost dear ones, who at Christmastime are very conscious of the one who is not there. Bless those who are poor, who are hurt by their poverty, not for their own sakes but for the sake of those gifts they long to give but cannot. Bless those who are ill and who must spend this time of joy in pain. Bless those who are far from home and far from friends, who are lonely and homesick among strangers in a strange place. Bless those who feel their loneliness and their loss more keenly in this time of fellowship and joy.

O God our Father, send thy Spirit among people this Christmastide. Make this a time when those who have quarreled will be reconciled. Make this a time when those who have drifted apart will find each other again. Make this a time when sons and daughters who rebelliously left home will come back home again and will find a welcome waiting for them.

O God our Mother, at Christmastime we give thee thanks for our greatest and best gift, Jesus Christ our Lord. We thank thee that he who is King of Glory entered into a humble home and took our common life upon him that he might make us what he is and that we in him might become thy sons and daughters.

Grant, O God, that at this Christmastime Christ may be born again within the hearts of each of us. This we ask for thy love's sake. Amen.   —*William Sloane Coffin Jr.*

Look upon us, O great Creator, with thy favor. As now we seek to realize thy presence, incline our wills and affections toward thee. Grant us the lowly heart which is the only temple that can contain the Infinite. May we learn, as so many have done before us, that the time of prayer is the time of renewal, when doubt is dispelled, hope revived, and faith quickened and confirmed.

We come to thee in penitence confessing our sins: the vows we have forgotten, the opportunities we have let slip, the excuses whereby we have sought to deceive ourselves and thee. Forgive us that we talk so much and are silent so seldom; that we are in such constant motion and are so rarely still; that we depend so implicitly on the effectiveness of our organizations and so little on the power of thy Spirit. Teach us to wait upon thee, that we may renew our strength, mount up with wings as eagles, run and not be weary, walk and not faint.

We bless thee for all thy bounties: for the world in which we live, the work thou hast given us to do, the lessons thou hast set us to learn. We praise thee for the great and simple joys of life: for the merriment and innocence of children, for the gift of humor and gaiety of heart, for the satisfaction of work attempted and duty done. We thank thee for the grace of Christ in common people: for their forbearance and generosity, their good temper, their courage and kindness; for the grace and strength of character which, wherever we find them, make it easier to believe in thee.

O God, who hast called our people to a position of trust and responsibility throughout the world, we thank thee for all the ways by which thou hast blessed and guided us unto this day. We confess before thee with shame all that has been evil in our history and all that even now makes us unworthy to be called a Christian people. Take from us, we beseech thee, all pride, greed, and injustice, and grant to us the spirit of unselfish service which alone can make us great.

Hear us when we pray for this country. Unite into one happy family the multitudes that have come hither out of many kindreds and tongues. Enable us to bear one another's burdens and to work together in concord, and may we use our liberties and privileges to promote the common good.

Hear us when we pray for this congregation. Prosper us in our labors, keeping our aims high and our motives pure. Deal graciously with those of our company who are in sorrow, sickness, or distress. Pour out thy Spirit upon all branches of the church. Grant that all who profess and call themselves Christians may be led into the way of truth and hold the faith in unity of spirit, in the bond of peace, and in righteousness of life.

All this we ask through Jesus Christ our Lord. Amen.

—*Robert J. McCracken*

Eternal Spirit, home of our souls, from whom we come, to whom we belong, and far from whom we have no peace, we worship thee. We who through another week have listened to the noisy voices of the world, listen now for thy still, small voice. Speak to us thine admonition, thy comfort, and thy hope.

Kindle gratitude within us lest we forget. Remind us of the homes from which we came, where some loved us better than they loved themselves; of our country which all our days has sustained us with blessings bought by other sacrifices than our own; of our friends through whose inspiration we are enabled to do what we ought to do and to endure what we must stand. Call to our minds great music, great books, great art, the spaciousness and splendor of thy natural world, where thou hast housed us like royal children in a palace, and above all thy greatest gift to us in Christ, that we may become humble and grateful.

Kindle within us sincere penitence. Let some austere word of righteousness be spoken to our consciences today. Save us from our mean excuses, our cheap defenses and low self-deceits. Give us grace to be honest with ourselves, that we may rightly judge our dealing with the personality thou hast entrusted to us, the friends with whom thou hast surrounded us, and the opportunities thou hast put before us. Stand us against the background of thy purpose for us in Christ, that we may be ashamed and penitent and transformed by the renewing of our minds.

Kindle devotion and loyalty in us. Send us forth from our worship not only comforted but empowered. Especially we remember our obligation to the oncoming generation of young men and women. Thou seest in our hearts the names of those we love in distant and dangerous places. O God, forgive us of older years who must turn over to them a world so bitter, so distraught. Make them wiser than we have been. Give them stronger hearts and wills and longer foresight. Grant them thy strong leadership, that they may hand on to their children a better world than this.

To that end empower thy church, set in the midst of this generation, to stand for faith and hope and love, while cynicism walks our streets and disillusionment looks in at our soul's windows and tragedy afflicts humankind. Deepen the church's devotion, we beseech thee. Quicken its faith, increase its wisdom; may it grow more inclusive, less dissevered and sectarian, more catholic and universal, and more rich in service, that it may be worthier of the high name of Christ it bears.

We remember before thee the nations of the world. O God, who in past times hast made even the wrath of humankind to serve thee, turn this present evil somehow into good. Save us now from our own insanity! Let not our greedy nationalism prepare once more wars, beyond this war, for our children to fight! In the presence of the sacrifice now being made by our youth on behalf of a decent world, we pledge ourselves with faith and patience and perseverance to work for righteousness and peace—in the spirit of Christ. Amen.

—Harry Emerson Fosdick

Epiphany

Eternal Spirit, we thy children, who through another week have presented our lives too much to the world to play upon, turn now to thee. Tune thou us to nobler music than the world has played upon us, we beseech thee.

If the ill behavior of others has begotten resentfulness in us, so that some of thy servants come to thy sanctuary bearing bitter and vindictive hearts, lift us up, we pray thee, into a nobler mood. Beget in us a larger tolerance, magnanimity, and goodwill that, thy love being shed abroad in our hearts through the Holy Spirit, we may be able even to forgive our enemies.

If the ill treatment of the world has discouraged us so that some of us come to thy temple with whipped and beaten souls, O Spirit of the living God, let thy fingers touch some strong chords of courage in our hearts today. Set us upon our feet again. Make men and women of us worthy of our parents, who in difficult circumstances have revealed the splendor of their spirits.

If some of us have failed and our own sins have shamed us so that we walk into thy presence with secrets in our souls that we would not have our friends know, O God, play, we beseech thee, upon our hearts by thy forgiveness and thy grace. If some of us within the houses and mansions of our spirits have hidden rooms from the thought of which we shrink and yet to which with fascinated imagination the footsteps of our reminiscences ever more are drawn, give us the grace of such repentance, such restitution to those whom we have wronged, such confession, if confession will do good, as shall restore us to thy favor and to our own self-respect. Blow through us, thou west wind of God, till all our skies be clear again and the sun shall shine once more.

If the world has played upon us with its prosperity and we bring happiness into thy sanctuary, watch us, O Spirit of God. Let not our happiness turn to frivolity and triviality and selfishness. Grant, we beseech thee, that every happiness we bring may become in this hour a blessedness also, and a benediction.

As thus we pray for our interior needs, we lift up before thee in the hands of our common intercession the civilization of which we are a part. For all the skill with which we have invented instruments to bring us material comforts we thank thee, but we bow before thee with humility and a deep consciousness of need for such inward wisdom and goodness that we may not ruin ourselves by the very instruments our hands have built.

Especially we pray thee for those upon whom the burdens of our new civilization rest heavily: the poor, the unemployed. Have mercy upon those for whom winter means only fear. And if we sit in privilege today, baptize our spirits with unselfishness and teach our hands service, that we together may bear the common burdens of this generation in this difficult time.

Bless, therefore, every institution of human service—all schools and colleges, all hospitals where the sick are lying, all churches, all those who sit in seats of government. And so, beyond our power to ask, minister to our needs this day privately and publicly, that the world through our worship may be lifted a little nearer to the doing of thy will and the satisfactions of thy peace. Amen.   —*Harry Emerson Fosdick*

Once again, O God, we gather to praise thy name that with all its sham and drudgery and broken dreams it is still a beautiful world. We thank thee for the blessings of the week just past, the days when we saw the sun overhead, the nights when we beheld the perfect silence of the moon and stars. We thank thee for all the snow that fell so that "the earth in solemn stillness lay." Yea, we would even thank thee for the cold and bleakness of winter, without which the warmth and splendor of spring could never be. So too we bless thee for the bitter medicine that heals, the misfortunes without which we could never grow wise or know the meaning of true joy.

In the coming week, keep us unfaltering, affectionate, faithful. And keep us humble, that we may continue to grow.

Hear now our prayers of intercession for those who are cold and hungry, that they may be satisfied; weary and heavy-laden, that they may find rest; for the rulers of the world, that they may be ruled by thee; for those who suffer wrong unjustly, that they may not be diminished by bitterness.

As a new year continues to unfold, bless us all, O God, with the sure knowledge that we are loved for ourselves and in spite of ourselves. So may we continue to love our world, to laugh at its sham, redeem its drudgery, and fulfill at last its broken dreams. All this we pray in the name of thy Son, Jesus Christ. Amen. *—William Sloane Coffin Jr.*

Eternal Spirit, from whom all things come and in whom all things consist, grant us, who are spirits, that we may worship thee, who art Spirit, in spirit and in truth. Thou art very great. Our imaginations cannot find thee out. Thy thoughts are not our thoughts, neither are thy ways our ways. Make us humble in our worship. Make us modest in our beliefs. Even when we face the outer world that our eyes behold and our hands handle, we are like children beside the sea, unable to infer its depths or understand its compass. How much more, then, art thou, O God, than our slender ways of thinking! How high art thou lifted up beyond our imaginations!

Yet save us from the discouragement of our inadequate thoughts concerning thee. For thou hast revealed thy quality to us. Thou hast spoken unto us in seers who have loved beauty and seen visions of goodness and truth. If we pluck up a drop out of the ocean, while it does not contain the depth and range of the sea's vastness, it still reveals the sea's nature. So we would dignify our little thoughts of thee, and rejoice that they are a revelation of the Eternal. So, once more, in the courts of thy sanctuary we would see the light of the knowledge of thy glory in the face of Jesus Christ.

We do not stand clamorously before thee in our petition, O God, as though reminding thee of things thou hast forgotten, or as though, better than thou art, we were pleading with thee to work righteousness and mercy that thou hadst not been good enough to work. Rather, we think of thee like the sun, whose nature it is to give, but whose giving is stopped too often by our shuttered windows. We would open ourselves to thee. If we are spiritually poor, it is our fault, not thine. Thou art rich. Oh the depth of the riches both of the wisdom and the knowledge of God! How unsearchable are thy judgments, and thy ways past tracing out! We would be responsive to thee. We would seek in thy presence the spirit of appreciation and appropriation and possession that we may be rich toward God.

We bring before thee our varied conditions and estates that we may see as in thy sight the problems of our lives.

We remember the needs of our bodies. Our God in heaven, who knowest that we have need of all these things necessary for the flesh, resolve our anxieties. If some here reading in thy word that they are not to be anxious, saying, What shall we eat?

or, What shall we drink? or, Wherewithal shall we be clothed? yet find themselves overridden and oppressed by their anxiety, we beseech thee that thou wilt help them. Thou canst solve our outward problems by giving us inward thoughts and new courage. Reconstruct our spirits as we face the difficulties of this present world. Give us a better point of view about our lives. Grant within us a new heart and a transformed mind, that here in thy sanctuary some dismayed and beaten souls may be inwardly rebuilt and sent out with new vision, fortitude, and wisdom to handle their lives.

We bring to thee the problems of our minds. O thou who hast told us that we are to love thee not only with all our hearts but with all our minds, we beseech thee that some light may break upon our thinking in thy house this day. Illumine some shadowed places. Let the radiance of thy wisdom shine upon some darkened, bewildered, and perplexed thoughts. Give us the clue to the labyrinth that we have missed. Thou resolver of riddles, clarify our thought.

We bring to thee the problems of our characters. Almighty God, dwelling in light unapproachable, canst thou know how much easier it is to see the ideal than to follow it, to understand duty than to do it, to behold the obligation of service than to fulfill it? Have mercy upon us, thy wayward and transgressing servants. We would rise this hour into one of our better moods. We would be lifted above our common placeness, elevated above our mediocrity, that in the high altitudes of the Spirit we may live this hour so well that we may go down refreshed in soul and lay hold on life once more with cleaner hands and purer hearts.

We bring to thee the problems of our friendships. For all those dear and deep relationships of life, where we are bound to one another in sincere affection, we pray thee. For fatherhood and motherhood, for the dear relationships of the marital life, for our sons and daughters, we pray thee. If today homes are represented here where a rift has begun, give guidance and comfort and a better temper. Save us all from that archtreachery, the betrayal of love. Give us elevation of spirit and wisdom of mind in dealing with our friendships. Lift up our appreciation of them even as we bow here. May all that is dear and excellent and beautiful in human life find new value because we have worshiped thee from whom all beauty comes, and send us out to be better friends because we have walked for a while in the friendship of Christ.

We bring to thee the problems of the great world of humankind. It is sometimes easier to believe in thee than to believe in people. As we look at the corruption of our lives, the squalor of our thought, the viciousness of our deeds, we are tempted to skepticism and cynicism, not so much about thee as about humankind. Reconstruct in us, we beseech thee, because we have worshiped here, a new faith in humanity. Help us to look upon men and women with something of the eyes of Christ. Thou Son of God and Son of Man, what did not we do to thee, even nailing thee to the cross, and yet thou didst believe in us, in our possibility and our destiny. Lift us up so to see others, we beseech thee, and so to have a new faith in humankind, that from this place we may go out restored in confidence that justice can conquer greed, that peace can overcome war, that love is stronger than hate, that life is mightier than death.

We ask it in the name of Christ. Amen.

—Harry Emerson Fosdick

Eternal God, beneath whose rule we live and in whose grace we stand, with all that is within us we would bless thy holy name. We thank thee for the constants in our life:

   that the ground is firm beneath our tread;
   that day follows night;

that the seasons march in predictable succession;

that the gates of mercy are ever open to us in our need.

We thank thee for all that is new and changing in our life:

for startling breakthroughs in the realm of science;

for the audibility of people too long silent and the visibility
of wrongs too long concealed;

for experimentation in the arts, and in particular the art of
public worship;

for new people next door or up the street, and the prospect
of contributing to one another's growth.

O thou whose ways are from of old and yet whose works are ever new, make us grateful for the past and open toward the future.

Through Jesus Christ our Lord.

We join our prayers to hold before thee this city of bright lights and broken hearts—a comedy to those who think; but to those who feel, a tragedy.

Grant to our mayor and those who share in governing the patience needed to contend with the clamor of competing voices and the ability to hear this clamor as the language of democracy.

Raise up in us, the people, the willingness to break with private goals often enough and long enough to ease some burden or to right some wrong.

Give us a new confidence in due process as a means of getting where we want to go, and the good sense to use our power, personal and conferred, with modesty and restraint.

Through Jesus Christ our Lord.

We pray now for ourselves, acknowledging that
    our lost radiance,
    our much fretting,
    our telltale tensions,
discredit the faith we profess and dishonor thee.
Renovate us, O God, through the tireless workings of thy Holy
Spirit, until all in us that is unworthy of the King may fall
away, and Christ rule unrivaled in our hearts.

Work thy will through us, O God. If not, thy will be done
through others.

All which we pray through Jesus Christ our Lord. Amen.

—Ernest T. Campbell

O God, whose graciousness is so far beyond our own, whose
goodness toward us is never-failing, help us stop trying to
prove ourselves. Let thy love for us, in the sight of all thy angels,
be so that we might sit loose to fame and fortune.

    Grant us to know that deepest joy which comes in respond-
ing to thy love with our own, by loving thee and by loving our
neighbor as ourselves. Amen.   *—William Sloane Coffin Jr.*

Lent

Ash Wednesday

Eternal God, praise be to thee for thy unwavering goodness to thy children.

> For mercies that fall like rain on the just and the unjust;
> for words that find us in our seasons of not-knowing;
> for songs thy love has taught our hearts to sing;
> for coincidental happenings which, viewed in retrospect, bespeak thy gentle leading and thy care;
> for good memories and true hopes, and every thought of thee.

We commend to thee this day those who stand in special need of prayer:

> all whose souls are hammered daily on the anvils of prejudice, and those who have broken with established social patterns to give them help;
> all who are aged and enfeebled, and those who hover round them like ministering angels;
> all who are disabled in mind or handicapped in body, and those who have taken their plight to heart and resolved to do them good;
> all whose lives are twisted by fear and superstition, and those who have gone to share with them the healing light of Christ.

For ourselves, O God, we find it hard to pray.
Well-clothed, well-housed, well-fed, well-served by gadgets
and conveniences, what lack we yet?

O thou who art holy beyond our telling, with whom we dare
not trifle:

> show us our poverty of spirit and the leanness of our souls;
> give us the will to search out new definitions of self-denial;
> teach our untaught hearts to love with a love like unto thine;
> curb our sloth;
> expose the timidity and unbelief that lie behind our craving
> for security;
> give us—in these days—to know, as we have not yet known,
> Jesus Christ in the power of his resurrection and the
> fellowship of his suffering.

These mercies we seek in faith and with thanksgiving, in his
name. Amen.   —*Ernest T. Campbell*

O God, from whom we come, to whom we go, in whom we live
and move and have our being, let the sense of thy sovereign
majesty take possession of our hearts and minds, that we may
humble ourselves in thy presence and offer unto thee a rev-
erent and adoring worship. We do not make our approach to
thee in fear and trembling as to a great and terrible judge but
as a child to its parent, knowing thy infinite love and care for
us and seeking, as we lift up our souls to thee, the inward tranquility that is both a sanctuary and a fortress.

   We make confession of our sins unto thee. Forgive us, that
even our prayers for pardon are perfunctory and casual; that
we acknowledge our offenses without naming them or resolv-
ing to have done with them; that we ask forgiveness without

shame and accept it without wonder; that we are satisfied with things as they are, in the church and in the world; that we lack moral passion and fail to share thy indignation with all that makes or loves a lie. Have mercy upon us. Correct us in our weakness, that we may love thee in thy strength. Wake in us a soul to obey thee not grudgingly or reluctantly but with joy and gladness. Sustain us in all the strictness of a disciplined life, yet show us that in thy service is perfect freedom.

We bring to thee the moral chaos of our world, its spiritual fatigue, its restlessness of heart, its dark forebodings. We acknowledge our share in the world's sin—our love of ease, our pride of race and place and possession, our hard bargaining and ruthless competition, our failure to take account of the needs of others. The vices of civilization are compounded of the lusts of us all. Work in us by thy grace a miracle of renewal and transformation. Grant us the strength of will to keep thy commandments and walk in thy ways.

Hear us when we pray for those who have dedicated themselves to the service of high and worthy causes: for all who are laboring for peace among the nations; for all who tend the sick and combat disease; for all who are engaged in the relief of the oppressed and the destitute; for all who seek the restoration of the broken unity of the church; for all who preach the gospel; for all who bear witness to Christ in distant lands.

We bring to thee the needs of this congregation, making special mention of those who are in bodily pain, or in sorrow of heart and home, or whose minds are bewildered and perplexed. Be compassionate and gracious to any here whom life has worsened—the sick of soul, the broken in will, the depressed and despairing. Show them anew the sources of strength and serenity, and fill them with joy and peace through believing.

Through Jesus Christ our Lord. Amen.

—Robert J. McCracken

Merciful God, because we love the world we pray now for grace to quarrel with it. O thou, whose lover's quarrel with the world is the history of the world, grant us grace to quarrel with the worship of success and power, with the assumption that people are less important than the jobs they hold.

Lord, grant us grace to quarrel with a mass culture that tends not to satisfy but to exploit the wants of people; to quarrel with those who pledge allegiance to one race rather than to the human race. Lord, grant us grace to quarrel with all that profanes and separates persons.

O God of mercy and hope, deepen, we pray, our faith so that we can remain our best when circumstances go against us. Resisting the temptation of melancholy, may we embrace the asceticism of cheerfulness, remaining tender, loving, and loyal to one another even as thou art tender, loving, and loyal to each one of us. We pray in the name of Christ. Amen.

—William Sloane Coffin Jr.

O Creator of all life—of the physical substance of existence, of energy, and of the spirit—we say our prayers to you to remind ourselves that the whole universe is yours, not ours, and that we too are part of that creation, but have been endowed with the gifts of choice, reason, and feelings for the purpose of being in your Garden and caring for it and determining its continuing creativity—or its destruction.

O God, so far that freedom has resulted in our making a shambles of this world. The greed and selfishness in us have trampled upon the earth, leaving behind dead bodies, twisted minds, and hatreds in the exploiters and the exploited that have lived for centuries.

Even now there are wars and political hostages, and there are those of us who are hostages to lies and evils that further the cause of injustice and brutality in the name of freedom.

Help us to understand that though you are ultimately in charge, you have given us dominion, and that if we are to live at all we must live together.

Help us to know that we cannot stand on the sidelines and watch the world go by. We must enter the struggle because you have given us the charge. Amen.   —*George Thomas*

God of yesterday, today, and tomorrow, the ceaseless Creator, revealed in every constructive act, we have come to the beginning of a new day, and we enter thy sanctuary to give thee praise for it. All around us nature is bursting into beauty and sound, celebrating the fact that the winter is over and new life springs up everywhere. Grant that our hardened hearts, huddled in their protective wrappings, may be sensitive to thy calling of new life and break through their shells into new growth. We bless thee for the life that has been given us already, for the glory of the lighted mind that can seek and know and order our lives, for the strength of heart that enables us to carry on when we would rather quit, and for the hope of soul that wakens in us courage for the morrow. We give thanks for all the tokens of thy unfailing love and presence.

And now, O God, we wait before thee. We have come because the world does not give us all we need. We come because we need to have our sights raised and our spirits lifted by understanding thy priorities for us. We come bringing the wants and desires for our own lives that we can never put aside for very long. Take us as we are, O God, and help us in these moments to be honest with ourselves and to know that your love, expressed in Jesus Christ, will more than make up for all our faults if we will just stop pretending to be righteous and let you use us as you will. Startle us into life, that we may be ready to receive new flashes of understanding and have our eyes opened to your wonder and glory.

Here in thy presence we know we cannot pray for ourselves without praying for others as well. Look down in mercy upon all who are in pain this day, those who are ill, those who suffer from anxiety of mind or bitterness of heart, those who endure loss or separation from loved ones. In the midst of their aching and fearful hours, may they find thy presence. Be with the lonely and unfriended, those who feel they must hide who they really are from those who would react in anger, those who must make hard decisions with no easy answers, those who find it hard to believe in goodwill when ill will is so much around them. Grant to those we love and who love us such a portion of thy grace and blessing as will keep them, and us, unto eternal life.

We pray for our unhappy world, with all its violence and wretchedness. Made to share this planet, we spend our efforts to be what we are not. We are enemies when we should be friends. When we stand before thee, we see of how little consequence are the divisions we have made—of race and color, nation and speech, class and creed. Our deepest human aspirations are the same; our deepest human needs are the same. Grant us not only to believe this but also to live it. Save us from living on a small scale in a great age.

Open the eyes of some of us here to causes that are worth giving our lives to. Though we may not see all things clearly, let us see some great things plainly and try to live by them. May the touch of Christ upon our spirits make us wise enough to help make our world a little better.

We pray in the name of Jesus Christ. Amen.

—Eugene E. Laubach

Passion Sunday

O God, how excellent is thy name in all the earth. One age declares thy goodness to another, and thy steadfast love is the mainstay of our ever-restless hearts.

We thank thee for the mystery of our years and the will to live;
>for the rewards of solitude and the pleasure of congenial company;
>for satisfactions that follow work well done and the renewing power of leisure.

We thank thee for hard choices that help us discover who we are;
>for goodwill from unexpected sources that find us in our seasons of depression;
>and for the gift of faith that makes thy love in Christ the broad and sure foundation on which we build.

Unashamed and unrestrained, we offer thee the tribute of our thanks.
>Through Jesus Christ our Lord.

Bless with thy power and presence, gracious God, those who do the menial chores and thankless tasks behind our city's bright facade:
>those who rise early to bring fresh food and produce from the marketplace;
>those who clean our halls and offices through the night;
>those who work our switchboards and see that messages get through;
>those who load and unload trucks;
>those who stock the shelves and work the back rooms of our stores;
>those who fire boilers and provide maintenance in the heat and noise of basements that we seldom visit;

those who clean our windows and mend our masonry and
   keep our flagpoles in repair;
those who set tables, bus dishes, and work in our many
   kitchens.

In following our several callings, make us aware of what we
owe to unnamed thousands whose work is indispensable to
our well-being. And give them to know, O God, that in thy
sight, if not in ours, the least of the earth are very big indeed.
   Through Jesus Christ our Lord.

As we near the hallowed ground of Gethsemane and Golgotha,
we confess to a sense of unworthiness and shame.
   Our deprivations are so few.
   Our scars so scarce.
   Our courage so seldom summoned.
   Our passion so wasted on self.
Who are we that we should bear thy name or purport to be
thy people?

Forgive us, O God, for we know not what we do.
   Expose the games we play with thee to stave off the moment
      of full surrender;
   and help us to come as the sinners we are, that we may
      obtain mercy and find grace to help in time of need.

Our prayers we offer in faith and with thanksgiving,
   through Jesus Christ our Lord. Amen.

—Ernest T. Campbell

Palm Sunday

Eternal God, who hast called us thy living temples, in whom
thou wouldst dwell, we would be worthy of thy habitation and
in our heart of hearts would set up an altar to thy praise. O thou

fountain of living waters, once more with thirst unslaked we come to thee to drink. We have tried to content ourselves with lesser things, but thou hast set eternity with in our hearts. We are restless until we rest in thee. Into the courts of thy sanctuary we would come with praise and worship and thanksgiving on our lips. Yet save us from the ancient sin of casting palm branches before thee at the week's beginning and crucifying thee before the week's end. Give us sincerity, we beseech thee. From the ungenuine lead us to the genuine, from the unreal to the real.

O thou who art of too pure eyes to behold iniquity and of too clear eyes to believe in our shams, pierce us and penetrate us with thy spirit, and grant that this day we may be laid bare to ourselves and to thee, and so may worship thee truly because we worship thee indeed. Give to us peace, O God. We are restless and irritated by life. Problems vex us, and the surface of our little pools is blown to anger and tumult by the winds of this present world. We seek serenity and tranquility, that for a time we may be still and know that thou art God. Sometimes our souls, thou seest, are like ancient chaos, and unless the Spirit of the living God brood over them, there shall be no order there.

Unite our souls this day in praise of thy name. Give us insight, we beseech thee. Too often we walk aimlessly, beat our way through the woods of life like children who have lost their path. O God, bring us to a clearing, lift us to a height, give us horizons, show us the clue, that henceforth we may walk meaningfully, that life may have significance and purpose for us.

O God, give us friendliness. We pray for pardon that so often saying thou art our Creator and we are all brothers and sisters, we yet live otherwise. We are teased and irritated by one another. Give us this day, we beseech thee, the Spirit of

God. Let the love of God be shed abroad in our hearts. Teach us the fine art of putting ourselves in others' places and seeing life as they must see it through their eyes, so that our irritation may pass into understanding and our vindictiveness into friendly desire to help.

O God of peace and plenty, who art able to strengthen us with thy Spirit in our interior selves, so deal with us this day that high business may be done for thy cause in our hearts, that we may go out from this place of meditation, prayer, and thought to be more worthy of our high vocation as thy children.

We beseech thee for the spiritual life of our nation and of the world. For all the benedictions that have come to us because we have had wit enough to master the physical world, we thank thee. For all the doors of opportunity that open before the human race this day, we thank thee. But, O God, thou seest how much easier it is for us to master physical nature than human nature. Control of the world without is much simpler than control of the world within. We pray thee for the spiritual life of humankind. Give us a keener conscience. Lift us up to a higher altitude. Deepen our care for righteousness, our respect for personality, and our love for all people.

To this end we beseech thee that thou wilt bless us in all the communities that are represented here. Send thy benediction upon our families. Especially bless all those at home from school and college who this day will eat at our tables and worship in our sanctuary. For their independence, for their adventurousness, for the nobleness of their lives, for their candor, for their love of reality, we praise thee. Save them from the liberty that becomes license, but keep us also from laying a dampening hand upon their ardor and a discouraging hand upon their love of adventure. God grant that they may find for this world a better way to walk in than their parents have found, who brought war and not peace.

We beseech thee that thou wilt cross the threshold of our lives this day. We face once more a reminiscent hour when Christ is recalled to us. Blessed be our God for him. In all our noblest hours we adore him. He is the beauty of thy face. He is the richness of thy life. He is the hope of the world. And as thus outwardly in the sanctuary we worship him, so we beseech thee that in our hearts we may be not conformed to this world but transformed by the renewing of our minds, that we may grow like him.

We ask it in Christ's name. Amen.

—Harry Emerson Fosdick

Holy Week

Maundy Thursday

Help us, gracious God, with open minds and contrite hearts to feel our way into the meaning of the arid mystery of this night:
>> quicken our imagination, to the end that what went on in that upper room may come alive for us.
>> For we would sit at table with the twelve and open ourselves to the close-up presence of the Christ.

"The Lord Jesus, the same night in which he was betrayed, took bread."
>> We marvel at the mastery of one who on the evening of his own demise could avoid all thoughts of self and bend to the task of breaking bread for others.
>> So strong in us is the urge to "get even" that we can scarcely fathom sharing food and drink with one whom we know intends to do us harm.
>> So brittle is our faith in the providence of God that we can only stand and stare when one whose ways are perfect shuns all complaining in his final hours and meekly asks thy blessing on the meal.

O God, we do not sit in judgment on the twelve for having hassled with one another over which was greatest, for pride has often marred our work for thee.

We are not surprised that one by one that night they asked, when betrayal was announced, "Is it I?";
>> For, like us, they knew full well that under ample provocation any one of them could cash their Master in!

Let this night be for us a night of resolution.

Bless us with a renewed and enlarged awareness of our need for grace:

> a more honest reading of our frailty and sin;
>
> a hope-building confidence in the durability of bread and cup;
>
> a stretching of soul as we contemplate a "foolishness" with thee that is wiser than our wisdom, and a "weakness" with thee that is stronger than our strength.

These prayers we offer in trust and thankfulness, through Jesus Christ our Lord. Amen.   *—Ernest T. Campbell*

Good Friday

O thou who art afflicted in the afflictions of thy people,

> we bow before thee in these holiest of hours, awed by the mystery of thy suffering love.
>
> That we should call this day Good Friday is a bafflement of language we can scarcely comprehend.
>
> And yet the highest good we know is strangely centered on that lowly hill to which our souls repair when other signs give out.

Blessed be thy name.

> Forgive us that with the cross as starting point we have made of Christian faith a bland and easygoing way of life.
>
> Forgive us that our preference runs to Bethlehem and Joseph's garden, to poinsettias and lilies,
>
> and away from Golgotha, with its rusted nails and twisted thorns.
>
> Forgive us that we are more willing to be instructed or reformed than we are to be redeemed.
>
> Open us, each one, to ever new and deeper meanings in our savior's passion.

Grant that we may never be casual before that event which
has taxed the skills of our finest poets and musicians,
rendered preachers mute,
and gained the grudging admiration and respect of those
with little time for thee.
Keep us, rather, reachable and pliable, responsive to grace,
willing captives of the wonder of it all.

Stir us now to such new intentions as will enable us to die to
self and live to Christ.
For, constrained by a love at once amazing and divine, we
would embrace a weary and despairing world and lift
that world to thee.

Through Jesus Christ our Lord. Amen.   *—Ernest T. Campbell*

Easter and Eastertide

Easter

Eternal God, the Alpha and Omega, who seest the end from the beginning, we worship thee. Once more in thy sanctuary we would be still and know that thou art God. Thou hast beset us before and behind and laid thy hand upon us, and in awe and reverence we would meditate upon the thought of thee.

We come in the spirit of thanksgiving, not most for the gifts which thou hast given us, although they are innumerable, nor for the deeds that thou hast done for us, although our hearts cannot calculate their richness. We thank thee first of all for thyself. Thank God for God! Blessed be thy name, that thou art at the center of our world, that thou dost bind it together and give it unity, meaning, and purpose. We adore thee. We rejoice in thee. We worship thee. Thou art the glory of our life. Without thee the world would be aimless and our life purposeless. O God, thou art God. Blessed be thy name.

We thank thee that thou art the God of Calvary, that thou hast taken the cross into thy understanding, that thou dost comprehend it. The cross of life is too deep for us altogether to know. It is very hard for us to bear. We thank thee that thou dost understand Calvary, that even though we do not know the explanation, there is an explanation and it is with thee.

Most of all, we thank thee that thou art this day a God of victory, and because we believe in thee we are awakened unto a lively hope that after every Calvary comes Easter Day and after every winter comes spring, that this corruptible must put on incorruption and this mortal put on immortality, and death be swallowed up of life.

For all the hallowed memories and the triumphant hopes that center in this day, we thank thee. For hate took love and buried it and, lo, love is returned to us triumphant. Death took life and made away with it, but life has risen from the tomb. Evil slew holiness, and holiness has come back to us again. Thanks be to God, who giveth us the victory through our Lord Jesus Christ!

We beseech thee that thou wilt save us from the formality that celebrates this day as an ancient event only. Waken us to an expectation of victory for our own lives. If beaten souls, whipped by persistent and pursuing sin, have come here to worship thee, give them a triumph today. Our habits bind us until we feel that though the strength of Samson were ours yet could we not burst the withes that tether us? Yet, O God, thou art the God of victory. Help us to rise triumphant over our sins.

Give us the triumph, we beseech thee, over our social evils. Many centuries ago, O Christ, thou didst come and teach, and on the mountaintop the sacred principles of thy holy faith were given to the world. Long ago thou didst die for us and rise again in triumph, and yet still thou dost see our inhumanity to one another. We confess our social sins, that our churches are but barely Christian, that our industries are but barely just, that our nations are unpeaceful and in love with war. Yet thou seest what high and beautiful faiths and expectations rise because thou art here. O Christ, thou hauntest the conscience of the world. From all hopelessness and cynicism, from all skepticism and lack of faith deliver us, good God, on this, thy Easter Day.

Give us the victory, we beseech thee, over our troubles. Thou seest the sorrowful hearts for whom Easter is clouded. We have stood beside the grave and the gravestone seems still to seal those whom we have loved better than ourselves. Bring them back to us this day, we beseech thee. Help us to worship here, a group not only of those who walk abroad on the face of the earth. Let the faces of those whom we have loved and lost awhile come back to us in memory this day, that the noble living and the noble dead may adore thee here together. The children who came up out of the gates of the dawn and could not tarry with us, the fathers and mothers who blessed our infancy and nourished us in the love of God and fell on sleep filled with high expectations concerning us, all beautiful friends who loved us better than they loved themselves—bring them back to us this hour, that we may sit with them in heavenly places in Christ Jesus.

O God, thou seest the heart of the whole world stirred this festival morning. Many a window that commonly is shuttered against thy light will be opened to thee on Easter Day. Let thy light come by many a strange path past many an impeding obstacle to multitudes of spirits over the whole world. Bring thy guidance and thy chastening. Make those that have been troubled serene, those that have been flippant thoughtful, those that have been faithless penitent, those that have been wicked pure, those that have been weak strong, those that have been desperate hopeful. Save thy people now, until the day dawns and the shadows disappear.

We ask it in the name of Christ. Amen.

—Harry Emerson Fosdick

O God, whose mercy is ever faithful and ever sure, who art our refuge and our strength in time of trouble, visit us, we beseech thee—for we are a people in trouble.

We need a hope that is made wise by experience and is undaunted by disappointment. We need an anxiety about the future that shows us new ways to look at new things but does not unnerve us. As a people, we need to remember that our influence was greatest when our power was weakest. Most of all, we need to turn to thee, O God, and to our crucified Lord, for only his humility and his strength can heal and free us.

O God, be thou our sole strength in time of trouble. In the midst of anxiety, grant us the grace to count our blessings—the simple ones: health, food, sleep, one another, a spring that is bursting out all over, a nation which, despite all, has so much to offer so many.

And grant us grace to count our more complicated blessings: our failures, which teach us so much more than success; our lack of money, which points to the only truly renewable resources, the resources of the spirit; our lack of health, yea, even the knowledge of death, for until we learn that life is limitation, we are surely as formless and as shallow as a stream without its banks.

Send us forth into a new week with a gladsome mind, free and joyful in the spirit of Jesus Christ. Amen.

—*William Sloane Coffin Jr.*

O Almighty God, we do not draw near to thee as those who fully know thee. We do not know thee aright. We know only in part. Thou art greater than that we should be able to comprehend thee with our thought. Thou art vaster and nobler than anything of which we have had experience. But we know what goodness is, and we believe that thou art good. We know what justice is, and we believe that thou art just. We know what love is, and we believe that thou art love. We know the qualities of thy nature, but what thou art in all thy infinite fullness we do not know.

We beseech thee to accept us, not because we profess to be able to comprehend thee but because we so sorely need thee. Thou art the source and center of our life. Thou hast made all things dependent upon thee for their existence, and thou hast made our hearts so that they are restless until they rest in thee. And yet, aware of this, we have been careless about that which should be our chief concern. We have taken little pains to establish a life of communion with thee. We have been slack in prayer and careless in living. We have not hungered or thirsted after righteousness. Have mercy upon us, O God.

Be pleased in thy great goodness to supply our need. Make us strong in body, clean in mind and imagination, upright in character and life. Help us to stand for the hard right against the easy wrong. Give us love of our work and of all duty to be done, whatever it may be. Amid all the strife and confusion of our time, preserve to us a vision of the world as thou wouldst have it be, and grant us some part in molding it nearer to thy purposes of love and grace.

Eternal God, in whose kingdom no sword is drawn but the sword of righteousness, and no strength known but the strength of love, show to the peoples of the world the things which belong to their true peace, that they may rise with a single voice to forgive past wrong, to repent present bitterness, and to remember their unity in thee. For those who are engaged in the government of this land, and for all who take council for the nations of the earth, we ask special gifts of wisdom and understanding, of patience and strength, that upholding what is right, and following what is true, they may hasten the coming of thy kingdom.

Deal graciously with all who are in any kind of distress. Be in every sad heart, in every stricken home, beside every bed of pain. Be with the weak to make them strong, and with the strong to make them gentle. Give comfort to those who are anxious in spirit, peace to those who are troubled in conscience, and the secret of victory to those who are in bondage to sin and fighting for deliverance.

Through Jesus Christ our Lord. Amen.

—*Robert J. McCracken*

Eternal God, thou fountain of life and thou light of human-kind, we turn once more unfilled and unillumined unto thee. Why should we have to seek thee, who art everywhere? Shall the birds fly to find the air and the fish swim far to seek the sea that we come into thy sanctuary to find thee, in whom we live and move and have our being?

Thou seest the insensitiveness of our hearts that keeps us in the ordinary day from thee, the dullness of our eyes that dims them so that we do not see thee in the common walk of daily tasks. Therefore we turn to thee to be found of thee and to find thee, thou Light of light.

See thou the things that we bring into thy sanctuary that we may understand them better and set them in their true perspective. We come with our blessings. We have been thoughtless of them. Often we have filled our lives with the smoke of our complainings and have made our friends unhappy when within our grasp were things beautiful, excellent, and of a good report, if we had understood. Help us in thy sanctuary to grasp again the virtue and beauty of appreciation. Open our eyes to see the benedictions within our experience this day. Grant us vision and insight, that we, who have been thankless when we should have been grateful, may cry once more because we have walked with thee, "Bless the Lord, O my soul!"

We bring our sins. We do not dare to leave them outside the sanctuary lest they meet us again when we go hence. We would bring them in with us; we would set them in the light of thy countenance. Help us to see them in their smallness, their meanness, in the selfishness that is their root, in the lamentable consequences that have been wrought on us and on our friends. Help us so to set them in the light of thy countenance and against the background of thy purpose and pattern in Christ that we may despise them, turn from them, sincerely repent of them. May high business be done in the souls of thy people because they have brought their sins with them into the sanctuary.

We bring our friends. They are to us very beautiful. They constitute for us the worth of life, for we are not the whole of ourselves; our friends are the rest of us. We would bring them into our worship. If some of them have passed through the experience that we call death, let that not keep them from meeting with us here. What is death to thee, O God, who canst see on both sides of it, thou God of the noble living and the noble dead? So we would keep company here this day with our friends, and worship thee.

We bring our hopes. Very mysterious to us is our life, O God. We did not ask thee to make us so. Thou hast made us. We roll the responsibility upon thyself. Thou hast called us into this strange life and given us not only memory and the present hour, but hope. Lift up our hopes, we beseech thee. Center them in fine things. Cherish in us noble aspirations. Fall upon us like the sun and the rain of springtime and bring all our fairest capacities into leaf and flower, that we may live in the future for those things most worth living for and may not spend our lives dropping buckets into empty wells and growing old in drawing nothing up.

As thus we pray for ourselves, we would not neglect the wide horizons of humanity's need. Far beyond our conscious understanding run the experiences of humankind. Of many colors, of many climes, of many racial backgrounds and traditions, we pray for them today. Our understanding is not deep enough, our sympathy is not fine enough, to comprehend them all, yet they are our brothers and sisters. We believe in one God; we must believe in one family. And so we lift them up in our poor prayers before thee, O thou who understandest before we ask what the world needs and who art not coaxed by our petitions to do something that thou hast forgotten. Flow thou down through our desires into the intermeshing network of this human family and, because we have prayed and thought and cared and loved this day, may the whole world be bound by gold chains closer to the feet of God.

Bind our churches one to another. Over the narrow definitions and sectarian allegiances that have dissevered us, help us to care for Christ and for the things Christ cared for. Lift up our nations into peace, and, after the long ages of our travail, let Christ yet see what his heart desired to see, what our saints have dreamed and our prophets prophesied, what our martyrs have died for and the cross of Christ was set up to achieve—the realm of righteousness and peace on earth.

We ask it in the name of Christ. Amen.

—*Harry Emerson Fosdick*

Pentecost

Our kind and gracious God, the hope of all who seek thee and the joy of all who find, diverse though we are in age and outlook, we are one in our desire to voice our gratitude to thee.

We thank thee for our time and place in history:
>for the vision of a better world, that even the baleful face of war cannot obscure;
>for the way in which our hearts keep finding in the Christ the master clue to what it's all about.

We thank thee for dormant passages of scripture that spring to life for us in crisis hours;
>for friends who mediate thy caring love;
>for the staccato thrust of new truth that raps on the door of our minds and will not take no for an answer.

All thy works praise thee in all places of thy dominion, and in that chorus we would gladly join.

Through Jesus Christ our Lord.

We pray on this day of Pentecost for the church wherever it is found. Open thy people anew to the empowering winds of thy Spirit, lest we look for sustenance to sources that were never meant to be our life.

Increase our confidence in the gospel as the word that makes us whole:
>our belief in the power of love to conquer hate;

our patience to accept and work through conflict as a way of
reaching peace;
our ability to be in the world but not of it.

Teach us to sing again, who can only cry.
Teach us to dance again, who are too much given to decency
and order.
Teach us to leap and run again, who have lost the first fine
careless rapture of our earliest years in Christ.
Let thy church, like a city set upon a hill, be a beacon of
hope and a sign of life for an age that seems to kill the
things it loves.
Bless thy church, O God,
with leaders who both think and feel;
with shepherds who love their sheep;
with theologians who balance faith and reason;
with members whose loyalty to Christ is a seven-day-a-
week affair for life.
Grant these mercies, we beseech thee.

Through Jesus Christ our Lord.

We pray, last, for ourselves:
a people who live in many different worlds;
a people capable of mischief and mercy;
a people who on clear days have seen forever and in dark
circumstances have struggled to see at all.
O God, cast us not away. For all our false starts and broken
promises, we love thee more than all.
Let the sick know that thou art God.
Be present through the watches of the night with those who
mourn.
Stay the impulsiveness of any who are toying with a self-
destructive act.

Revive us, O God, in the midst of the years, and let something of thy beauty be upon us. For we would live even as we pray, to thy praise alone. Through Jesus Christ our Lord. Amen.

—*Ernest T. Campbell*

Trinity Sunday

Eternal Spirit, high over all, blessed forever, whose dwelling is the light of setting suns, the round ocean, the living air, the blue sky, and, in our minds, we worship thee. In thee we live and move and have our being, yet we apprehend thee not. Thou art closer to us than breathing and nearer than hands and feet, and yet we understand thee not. Thou speakest unto us in all the goodness, beauty, and truth we know, and yet we debate thy being as though birds should argue the air they live in. O God, be not thus vague to us. Make thyself real. Unveil our eyes. Make sensitive our hearts, that we may feel. Challenge us in conscience. Allure us in ideals. Speak to us through minds that see the orderliness of thy universe and hearts that love goodness, and grant that this day we may have an answer to our prayer: Lord, we believe; help thou our unbelief.

Make the divine life real, we beseech thee, in our homes. Blessed be God, who settest the solitary in families! For benedictions that have streamed upon us from fathers and mothers who loved us better than themselves, we thank thee.

Make the divine life real in our churches. So long ago at Pentecost thy power came down upon a discouraged band of thy disciples, who went out to overthrow the world. Let not their work fail in our hands! Baptize us once more with the Spirit. We have grown prosperous; we have built great institutions; we have achieved worldly power. We are not despised and rejected. We are tempted to pride. Let not Pentecost fail within us! Renew the inner Spirit of the Christ in thy church,

O God; his humility, his meekness, his generosity and good-will, his boundless care for all personalities, his freedom from narrow prejudice, the breadth and magnanimity of his inclusive spirit, that thy church may be worthy of his name.

Make the divine life real, we beseech thee, in our societies. We repent before thee, O God, with sadness of heart. We repent for the cruelty of mobs who burn and slay without justice and without mercy. We repent before thee the unemployed who walk our streets and the poverty that lurks in the deep shadows of our bright prosperities. We repent before thee all wars and rumors of war, where we forget nothing of ancient hatreds and learn nothing concerning the evils of mutual slaughter. Yet beneath all the wrong that bows down our hearts with shame and penitence, we see the forward movement of thy purpose through the ages. Clothe our hearts with a new courage. Strengthen our wills with a new determination. Lure us with a fresh vision. Send us forth to make the divine real in our societies.

Make the divine real in our private lives. O God, out of what varied circumstance we come to worship thee thy searching and penetrating Spirit alone can know. For some of us are young and some are old, some of us are rich and some are poor. Upon some the benediction of unbroken family circles rests, and some have lately laid their dead away and beside the grave have cried, "How empty are my arms!" Some are happy and some are vexed and irritated, storm tossed, and anxious, and full of fear. O God, lift upon us all, we beseech thee, the peace of thy saving Spirit. Let us grow quiet in thy presence. Let tranquility, serenity, and calm take the place of pride and anxiety, vexation, and fear. Let all that is worst in us sink. Let all that is best in us rise. Give us an hour when we dwell upon the heights and make new acquaintance with the loveliest we know. Make Christ real to us, and, because we have dwelt for an hour in his presence, may we go down wiser to solve our problems, stronger to do our duties, and lovelier to live with.

We ask it in the Spirit of Christ. Amen.

—*Harry Emerson Fosdick*

O Creator God, we return thanks to thee for all thy revelations which in times past have been sacraments to our souls. Once more thou hast opened the gateway of another morning, and the glory of the earth comes through it. Lift up our hearts to praise thee. Make nature a sacrament to our souls. Let it speak to us not of itself only but of the eternal artist on whose palette all colors have been mixed.

We thank thee for the revelation of thy church, for that invisible fellowship of the sons and daughters of the Spirit, who, across the generations, have kept the great tradition of goodness and truth. Many have been their names, various their beliefs, but at the center of their souls shone a great light, and by it thou hast made all the world more beautiful. Join us to their company. We rejoice in the music through which they have praised thee and the books in which they have written their thoughts of thee. We rejoice in the deeds by which they have revealed thee and lifted the earth nearer to the kingdom of righteousness. We rejoice in the lives that, in their inner purity and truth, have stood for thee in scorn of consequence. Lift us up, we beseech thee, to be members of their company, and let the benedictions of the gospel of peace fall upon our souls this day. Thus we would retreat from the sordidness of life, from its din and its passion, from its hectic business and its superficiality, and find once more our confident resource, our security, our tranquility, our peace, and our power, in thee.

Deepen our faith this day. Give us a new grasp of the things unseen and eternal. Save us from being the slaves of our eyes and believing only what they see. Help us to understand that through the veil of the visible the meanings of life must come, invisible, eternal, spiritual. Quicken our hopes this day. Save us from the current cynicism of the generation in which we live, from its skepticism of things beautiful and its disbelief in the possibilities of human life. Lift us up above its derogatory and condemning attitude that would kill all things that are right and make impossible anything that is lovely. Heighten our hopes, and send us out believing once more that in the heart of humankind are possibilities which the touch of the living God can quicken into reality.

Expand our love this day. O God, transcend our selfishness. Help us to rise above our hatefulness, our vindictiveness, our prejudice, and our provinciality. If any of us have brought hate into this house today, may we find it flowing from us because the love of God has been shed abroad in our hearts.

We beseech thee, O God, for all hopeful and constructive movements now afoot in human life. We pray thee for all scientists seeking truth, for all teachers trying to guide the minds of the coming generation, for all physicians at work in the hospitals, for all those who love beauty and seek to create it, for all philosophers who endeavor to cast light upon the deep problems and mysteries of human life, for all servants of the common good who in sincerity and truth are endeavoring to lift this low-lying humankind of ours up to the realm of peace.

Especially we beseech thee for the schools and colleges from whose doors pour the multitudes of our boys and girls. We of the older generation repent before thee that we must hand over to them this earth so riven with superstition, so cursed by falsehood, so bitter in its spirit, so stained with the blot of war. God grant that the hands of the new generation, receiving this earth from us, may carry it to better days, and so grant upon them clarity of vision and seriousness of purpose and abounding faith.

We beseech thee for the deep and unspoken needs that have been brought into this sanctuary of prayer this day. Go thou deep into the hidden corners of our hearts. If there are unforgiven sins there, grant us true penitence, that thou mayest pardon them. If there are weaknesses there which, unknown to us, may yet cause our downfall in our own eyes and the ashamed sight of others, give us knowledge of them, that we, being made strong where we are weak and given power where we are frail, may come off more than conquerors. So not according to our merits but according to the riches of thy goodwill and wisdom, minister to us this day in the deep places of our hearts.

We ask it in the name of Christ. Amen.

—Harry Emerson Fosdick

Almighty God, the God and Father of our Lord Jesus Christ and in him our Parent also, we lift up our prayers unto thee. Thou art never far from any one of us, for in thee we live and move and have our being. But when, as now, we assemble in thy house, listen to thy word, sing the great hymns of aspiration and faith, we feel upon us thy quickening touch.

We thank thee, because when the fullness of the time was come thou didst send Jesus to reveal thy mind and will. In him we trace thy likeness and know what thou wouldst have us be. In his life of service and self-denial, of strength and joy, we see the end and goal of all our striving; in his passion and death we see the unconquerable love by which our sin is purged away, and we turn in penitence and gratitude to thee; in his resurrection we see the triumph of thy goodness over all the forces of evil.

Let his Spirit take possession of us, speaking in our words, thinking in our thoughts, working in our deeds. We remember his patience and considerateness; his disregard of his own comfort and convenience; his devotion to thy will; his insight and sympathy; his concern for the good of humanity and for thy glory. Let the same mind be in us that was in him. Show us what he knew so well, that thou hast need of us to fulfill thy purposes for the world and that we have need of thee if life is to be rich and full and satisfying.

O God who knowest the trouble we are in by reason of our unhappy divisions, give wisdom and grace to those who are laboring for understanding between the nations and to all who are seeking to break down the dividing walls between Jew and gentile, bond and free. Awakening to thy command, may thy people go forth in self-denying service, yet in great might, to win humankind to the love of thy name. Pour out thy Spirit upon this congregation, that to all its members there may come a new vision, a new consecration, a new companionship with Christ.

Look upon us now with thy favor. Draw near in sustaining grace to those who are beset by temptation, burdened by a sense of guilt, worn by anxiety, enduring bereavement, facing ill health or adversity or any kind of trouble. Let thy life flow into ours to cleanse, to heal, to renew. In the Spirit of Christ we make our prayer. Amen.   —*Robert J. McCracken*

O God, may we find you in all of life—in the trees, in the rain, in the air, in the earth—in everything that breathes your breath of life. And especially may we find you in ourselves and in others. May we reach out to kindred spirits, our brothers and sisters, whose divinity like ours is clothed in humanity, whose nature like ours is both good and evil, whose will like ours does that which it should not do and neglects that which it should do.

Help us to move with you toward your kingdom on earth and to remember that this movement toward justice and mutuality and caring for all life requires not only personal change but also the transformation of those economic, social, and political structures and institutions which in part shape the ways we feel and think.

Help us to remember that the things of this world are not ends in themselves but means by which your will, your purposes, and your Spirit can be realized on earth. Hear us now as we identify our oneness, and renew your covenant with us. Amen.
                                                              —*George Thomas*

Eternal Spirit, from whom we come, to whom we belong, and in whose service is our peace, we worship thee. Very mysterious is this universe into which, without our asking it, thou hast ushered us—we stand in awe before power beyond our thought to measure, distances that stagger our imaginations, questions that we cannot answer, and problems that we cannot solve. Very mysterious is our life within us, that from the freshness of its April passes to the cold of its December and is rounded by a sleep.

Lift us up, we beseech thee, from ingratitude to thankfulness. Strangely commingled is our life of things good and evil, happy and unhappy. Various and inconstant are our fortunes here. Forgive our eyes their tendency to seek the dark and troublous things. Forgive our imaginations that they fashion our lives into anxiety and gloom and so absorb us in fears and forebodings that we think of little else. Grant, we beseech thee, an hour of saner perspective and truer horizon. Let memory be our sacrament. Rekindle within us the fires of thankfulness. Remind us of homes where beauty dwells, of children that rejoice our hearts, of friendships that bless us, and of traditions from times past for which others have shed tears and paid the price of sacrifice. Tune our spirits once more to gratitude.

Lift us up, we beseech thee, from cowardice to courage. Save us from self-pity. Recover us from our whimpering complaints. Lo, we are the sons and daughters of soldiers who fought a good fight before they fell on sleep and were not afraid. Build into us also stout hearts, that we in our generation may stand undaunted by fear, unconquered by adversity, untainted by cowardice.

Lift us up, we pray thee, from vindictiveness to goodwill. If we are harboring a grudge, if hatefulness has taken hold of our spirits, save us, we pray thee, from such a desecration of this holy hour. Bring sympathy back to us, and understanding and the fair grace to put ourselves in others' places before we judge them. Lift us up above malice and evil-speaking and unkindness of heart. Arouse in us the spirit of Christ, who could pray upon the cross for those who put him there. O God, help us to be Christians in our hearts because love is there.

Lift us up, we pray thee, from selfishness to service. Remind us of downcast and stricken lives. Let our imaginations run out into our prisons, the houses where the poor lie down in cold and penury, the asylums where disordered minds beat themselves out against their vain imaginings, the unprivileged areas of our city's life and of the world where blessings that we take for granted are little known, and hunger stalks and fear haunts and tomorrow is full of terror. Wake up within us, we beseech thee, our forgotten kindliness. Help us, we pray thee, to make operative our Christian spirit. May multitudes be happier because, praying for this, we have gone forth to do it.

And with all this, Spirit of the eternal Christ, lift us up from doubt to faith. Lift us out of our cynicism, our skepticism, our unwillingness to believe that the good may be true, into a courageous faith and certitude concerning God and divine purposes. Illumine us, thou Sun of the morning, until not only shall our mountain peaks shine with a new confidence, but the very valleys shall feel thy noontime's splendor and we shall have faith again in ourselves, in others, and in thee.

We pray in the Spirit of Christ. Amen.

—*Harry Emerson Fosdick*

O God, who dwells in high places and yet also in the hearts of those who are humble, we are gathered once again gratefully to acknowledge that thou hast been our shepherd. We have not wanted! As our cup has overflowed, so now do our hearts.

We know, O God, that beauty is everywhere, just as suffering is, and we would become experts in the art of discovering beauty in every person—ourselves not excluded.

We bless thee for those who pitch tents of light in the dark valleys of this world; for those who refuse to give up; for those who know that peace is never so wild a dream as those who profit by its postponement pretend; for all those who stretch out tender hands to hearts and bodies in pain.

Grant, O God, that we too, in the week ahead, may not lose heart. Make us realize that beauty is always at hand and that from thee and from one another, as from earth and sky and all that walks and all that flies, we may derive strength and joy and endless pleasure. Hear the gratitude of our hearts. Amen.

—*William Sloane Coffin Jr.*

O almighty God, lead us into the blessedness of the mystery of communion with thee. As we bow in reverence before thy infinite majesty, lift us up into a sense of kinship with thy self. Send the spirit of thy Son into our hearts, that from the heart we may call thee our Father and our Mother. Bestow upon us the peace which quiets every misgiving and the trust which fills the soul with joy and gladness. Save us from the emptiness of a hurried life and from the frustration of a sinful one. Since we so readily forget that it is so, remind us that we cannot have the consolations of faith without its commitments, and that its delights are known only to those who have imposed upon themselves its disciplines.

For the daily gifts of thy providence we thank thee—for every blessing of soul and body; for the work thou hast given us to do and the strength with which to do it; for the comfort and happiness of our homes and the sanctities of family life; for everything in the world around us that speaks to us of thee and helps us to see the beauty of holiness. Above all we thank thee for Christ, the greatest of thy gifts to us, with whom thou dost freely give us all things and in whom all good and perfect gifts are comprehended.

We commend to thee this nation and all the nations. We pray that the peoples of the world may be kindled with that fire which Christ came to cast on earth and be filled with a conquering passion for peace; that the leaders and governments of the world may have the vision and the courage boldly to seek peace and perseveringly to ensure it; that individuals and nations may be prepared to make sacrifices for the sake of a just and durable order as readily as they made sacrifices in time of war, until suspicion, mistrust, fear, and hatred are banished from the world of God our Creator; that the hope of a brighter day and a better world may bring comfort to those whose homes and hearts have been broken by war.

O God, who willest not that any should live without comfort or die without hope, have compassion on the multitudes in many lands who are oppressed by bitter poverty. Bless and direct those who are working for their relief. Watch over the children, the sick, the aged. Rouse the careless, inform the ignorant, restore the fallen. Stir the conscience of the peoples, O God, and break the rule of covetousness and greed. Make plain the way of deliverance, and hasten the time when sin and shame shall no more have dominion over us. In the spirit of Christ we pray. Amen.   —*Robert J. McCracken*

Eternal Spirit, high above all yet deep within us all, we turn our hearts to thee. All our thoughts touch but the outskirts of thy ways; our imaginations are but partial pictures of thy truth; our words concerning thee are short plummets dropped into a deep sea. Incomprehensible, infinite, almighty, all-wise, how unsearchable are thy judgments, and thy ways past tracing out! Yet into thy sanctuary we come with grateful and expectant hearts, because while we, by searching, cannot find thee out, thou, by thy searching, canst find us out.

Spirit of the living God, discover us today. Come through the tangled pathways, grown with weed and thicket, that have kept us from thee. We cannot reach to thee; reach thou to us, that some soul, who came here barren of thy grace, may go out, singing, "O God, thou art my God!"

Discover us in conscience. Let some moral imperative be laid upon our souls today. Save us from our evasions and deceits, and the soft complacency with which we excuse ourselves and let some ennobling word of justice and beauty come to us today. Be stern with us, O living God, and chasten us by strong guidance in righteousness.

Discover us through the experience of forgiveness. Thou seest how many sins here have never been made right—words spoken that hurt another, never atoned for, and still unforgiven, wrongs done, and no restitution made. Grant the salvation of forgiveness that we, forgiving others, may be forgiven. May some friendships gone awry be put straight today, some broken relationships be gathered up again into purity, loveliness, and peace, because thou hast discovered us.

Come to us in the spirit of dedication. Carry us out of ourselves; save us from our self-centeredness. Never great until we confront something loftier than our own lives, never happy while we are self-centered, we seek our salvation in thee. Bring thou within our ken some purpose worth living for; remind us of someone whom we can help, some cause that we may serve! May we forget ourselves into character and usefulness, because thou hast found us out.

Come to us in the experience of inner power. Thou seest how in fancied self-sufficiency we have impoverished our lives. Face us with the truth that no great living can be based on pride. We ask not for easy lives, but for adequacy. We ask not to be freed from storms, but to have houses on rocks that will not fall. We pray not for a smooth sea, but for a stout ship, a good compass, and a strong heart to sail. O God, discover us with the resources of thy power, that we may be strong within.

Ah, God, who thus canst find us out, seek out our unhappy world in all its wretchedness and violence. See how our sins have wrecked the peace of humanity, divided us into warring nations and hostile races, and made so unequal our comfort and estate that the world is rent by envy and ill will. Come thou to thy wayward humanity, all of us thy children, one family with one God, trying ruinously to be something that we are not, enemies when we should be brothers and sisters. Bring the spirit of the Christ into our hearts, we humbly beseech thee. Amen.   —*Harry Emerson Fosdick*

O God, who art above us and in us and through us, we come to worship thee, seeking a fresh consciousness of thy reality and thy penetrating presence. We want to move past mere talk about thee and discussions about thy attributes. We would not argue, but would experience thee now.

We praise thee for thy never-ending presence, which surrounds us with thy love, which strengthens us in our weakness, and which guides us in our perplexity. We bless thee for thy patience with us in spite of our willfulness, for the sense of providence in our lives, and for all the assistance and direction of thy Spirit's leading.

O thou who didst brood over the world at its beginning and bring order out of chaos, brood over the human situation now, and bring order from the chaos among nations. Encourage every impulse to peace; empower those who lead and those who follow to build a world that does not rest on force but upon the concern for the common good of all. May the travail and storms of our time help purge the earth of its evil.

We pray for this church, which is thine and ours. Surrounded as we are by worldliness and indifference, give us faithful obedience to the surety that with thee alone is life. Deliver us from doubt and disillusionment, from cynicism and rebellion. Though we may not see all things clearly, help us to see some great things plainly, that we may live by them. Draw us together as a community of tender and forgiving people.

Be where people hurt; be where people are healing. Bind the broken hearts; help mend the torn bodies and ease the disturbed minds.

In the presence of our daily work, when there seems so little space for quiet, help us to remember thy Son, our Lord, who knew neither impatience of spirit nor confusion of work, but in the midst of all his labors kept a tranquil heart. Amen.

—*Eugene E. Laubach*

O God, who art always near to us, but especially near when we seek thy face in prayer, open our eyes that we may see thee, and our ears that we may hear thee, and quicken our hearts that they may become responsive to thy touch.

We bow before thy sovereign majesty in humility and awe. Great art thou and greatly to be praised; marvelous is thy power, and thy wisdom is infinite; wonderful are thy works in creation and redemption; wherefore we praise and we magnify thy name.

For all the kindnesses thou hast bestowed upon us we gratefully thank thee. Thou hast vouchsafed to us so many proofs that thou carest for us. Thou hast been about our path, considering all our ways and encompassing us with the blessings of thy goodness. Thine eye has been upon us to deliver us from evil and to be our help and shield. Thou hast instructed and taught us in the way that we should go and hast continually guided us by thy counsel.

Forgive us, we beseech thee, our many sins. We have lived in this world and forgotten that it is thine. We have received thy gifts and ignored the Giver. We have been selfish and self-centered; have made life minister to our own ends and purposes; have forgotten that those who seek to save their life lose it while those who surrender it in service and sacrifice find the abundant life.

O God, who knowest the burdens we bear and the temptations that beset us, grant us the royalty of inward happiness and the composure which comes from living near to thee. Daily renew in us a sense of joy, and let thy Spirit dwell in our hearts, that we may carry around the infection of a good courage and may meet all life's ills and accidents with gallant and highhearted happiness, giving thee thanks always for all things.

O God, the Physician of all people and nations, look upon the distractions of the world and the divisions of the church, and be pleased to stretch forth thy hand in healing. Prosper all those organizations and institutions which are working for a better understanding among human beings and for a just and durable order of society. Deliver us from pride and arrogance, from violence and discord. Endue with the spirit of wisdom all to whom is entrusted the responsibility of government.

O loving Creator, we pray for all on whom is laid the cross of suffering: the sick in body and the distressed in mind. Comfort all who mourn the loss of those dear to them. Give them faith to look beyond their sorrow to the reunion of souls in thy kingdom which is for ever and ever.

Through Jesus Christ our Lord. Amen.

—*Robert J. McCracken*

O God, who while we rest neither slumbers nor sleeps, whose pain passeth all understanding, we thy creatures bless thee, for yet another gorgeous day has been granted us, whose beauty and goodness we hope not to miss.

Once again we pray for thy help, not that we might do greater things, but that we might do better things; not that we might be spared life's pain, but that we might become wise; not that we might have all things to enjoy life, but that we might be grateful that thou hast given us life to enjoy all things.

Teach us, O Father, that gladness is always at hand.

Teach us, O Mother, that contentment lies always in discerning the value of things we have.

O Jesus Christ, who bleeding, broken, bowed, yet unconquered, still reigns from the cross, touch all our hearts this morning with the fire of your love, that we may run and not grow weary, walk and not faint, until we can say of our world what we can gratefully say of this day: beautiful, beyond any telling of it! Amen. —*William Sloane Coffin Jr.*

O God, slow us down and help us to see that we are put in charge of our lives, but with thy help. Help us to get in tune with the rhythm that makes for life.

We keep moving, even though we know that we are made to center down, as well as to be actively engaged in the business of life. We compete for things and make those things more important than they ought to be. We eat what we ought not to eat. We neglect and misuse our bodies. We fail to discipline our minds and to be still and know that thou art God and that we are the temple of the Most High. Yet we often complain about our misfortunes and our hard luck, when at times it is we who are guilty of disregard.

Help us to know that we can be broken by life only if we first allow the victory of evil over our spirits.

May our hope and strength and faith be grounded in you; and may we recall the strength of our model, our brother and your Son. Amen.   —*George Thomas*

Let it not be, O God, that praise should rise to thee from all places of thy dominion while we hold our peace. Charge our being with the currents of gratitude, that whatever be our momentary mood or fortune, we may find cause to bless thy name.

We thank thee for patience that helps us bridge desire and fulfillment;

    for unwise prayers that went unanswered, sparing us heavy pain;

    for the unwelcome new that led us to discover in ourselves capacities we never dreamed were there;

for ancient words of scripture that blaze with light and meaning as our circumstances change;

for the winsomeness of Jesus that excites the trust of young and old in every generation;

and for thy mercy that holds us fast even when we are hardly worth the holding.

Let the joy of what thou art indwell our souls, that even in the worst of times our hearts may sing thy praise.

Through Jesus Christ our Lord.

We pray today for those among us, and in the world around us, who are burdened not by too little but by too much:

those who have so much power that they have grown indifferent to the rights and claims of others and are fast becoming what they do not wish to be;

those who have so much health that they cannot understand the sick or reckon adequately with their own mortality;

those who have so much wealth that they prize possessions more than people and worry into the night about losing what they have;

those who have so much knowledge that they have grown proud and self-sufficient and lost the common touch;

those who have so much virtue that they cannot see their sins or appreciate thy grace;

those who have so much leisure that they move like driftwood on the surface of existence, lacking any cause larger than themselves.

O thou who art able to save us from abundance or privation, meet the strong in their strength. Possess them in the fullness of their powers, that what they have and what they are may be conscripted for thy service, wherein is peace.

Through Jesus Christ our Lord.

With yearnings that we cannot fully identify, much less describe; with fears too personal to voice; harboring hostilities of which we are ashamed; and weighted with a sense of guilt for having done so little with so much; we make bold now to pray for ourselves:

> teach us what it means to live in thee,
>> to rest in thee,
>> to hope in thee;
> let thy presence fill those homes where death has come;
> let thy wisdom fall like a gentle rain on the parched souls of all who are confused;
> let thy warming, healing light kindle trust in those who are sick or in any way afflicted;
> let thy joy overcome the dolefulness of those who have forgotten how to laugh.

Shape thy grace around our inmost needs, O God. Give us not over to ourselves. Strive with us yet a little longer, for we love thee and would serve thee fully.

> Through Jesus Christ our Lord. Amen.

—Ernest T. Campbell

Eternal God, from everlasting to everlasting, the Alpha and Omega of this vast creation, making unity of its diversities by thy purpose and thy power, we worship thee. We worship thee because we also would be made one. From all the dispersion of our random living we would be called together, unified, and integrated. Thou canst take this vast and varied universe and make us think of it as made by one Power and sustained by one Providence. For all its earthquakes that stun us with awe and its little children that awaken us to tenderness, we say that thou art one. O God, unify our diverse lives. Bring them together. Make unity and peace out of their confusion. And against all that divides them, scatters them, and makes them futile with confusion, we pray thee this day.

Give us purposefulness, we beseech thee. Forgive us for our aimless living, for all the random dispersion of our lives in things that matter little or not at all. Help us to discover once again something in life so worth the soul's devotion that all our existence shall be drawn together around a central loyalty.

Give us faith, O God, faith in something so beautiful and good that our lives will be drawn into unity by our vision and love of it. Save us from cynicism, from skepticism, from all those maladies of the mind and moods of the spirit that spoil our lives, and help us this day to see a vision of something excellent and august, beautiful and elevated, that we may believe in it and so be unified.

Give us love, O God. Bestow upon us the fine gift of friendliness. Forgive us for the way we tear our lives apart with our angers and our hatreds, our grudges and our vindictiveness. Teach us once more, Spirit of the Christ, that when we hate we do ourselves more harm than we do our enemies. Draw us together into unity because thou plantest goodwill at the center of our lives. As thus we pray for those forces that draw our lives together and against those evils that scatter them in a careless, random living, so we pray for those powers that draw our societies together. God, forgive us for the prejudices and hatreds whereby we have cut asunder our humanity and have made of what might have been an earthly paradise a hard and bitter place.

Especially we beseech thee for those forces that unite our nations, for every cause that works for goodwill and peace, for justice and a sound mind. Against all that divides us, against all that is hateful and provincial, against all policies of selfish isolation, against all grudges that cut like a sharp knife through the cooperation of humanity, we pray thee, and we beseech thee that thy benediction may so rest upon those who think and those who plan for peace that, for as long as the forces of war, well-organized, have wrought havoc upon this earth, so the forces of peace, being organized, may bring tranquility.

We pray thee for the union of our religions. Teach us ever with deeper and more sympathetic insight to look below the surface into the hearts of all who worship God. O God, thou seest that, all alike, we share in the heritage of old superstitions, that we all have come up out of the dark, that we all need thy chastisement and guidance, thy cleansing and power as we seek to worship God and serve others. Below all our differences teach us our commonality. Beyond all our varieties teach us our common goal. And so bring together, we beseech thee, upon this planet the spiritual forces that ought to make for peace, that religion, no longer dividing humankind, may yet unite us in the cause of humanity, and thee.

Cross now all those inner thresholds that so often keep our best friends from our secret lives. Minister thou to our several needs. In bereavement comfort us; in hardship sustain us. We ask in the name of Christ. Amen.   *—Harry Emerson Fosdick*

Gracious God, whose presence is felt in all the sights and sounds of ear and eye, we come to thy house to give thee thanks and praise.

From a world whose people know thee not and serve thee not, we come. From a nation whose people have forgotten their purpose and destiny, we come. From homes where we profess to love thee but do not show it in our dealings with others, we come.

And here we would be thy church. Strengthen us; show us the path that is ours to walk and work that is ours to do. Forgive us; let not memories of past failures dominate our service in the present. Give us such an awareness of thine all-encompassing love that in all times and in all seasons and all circumstances we may know thou art our God. Amen.

—Eugene E. Laubach

O God, whose love is unfailing and whose mercies are new every morning, in this house of prayer hallowed for us by thy presence, we lift up our souls unto thee. Grant to each one of us what thou hast made us to long for—cleansing from selfishness and sin, release from anxiety and fear, a life touched to finer issues and saved from futility by its devotion to goodness and to thee.

We thank thee for everything that speaks to us of thee—the beauty of these autumn days, the affection and constancy of our friends, the inspiration of great music and good books, and especially for the revelation of thyself in Jesus Christ and for the sending of his Spirit into our hearts.

Let that Spirit become regnant in our lives, delivering us from indolence and sloth, from depression and disloyalty, from misuse of thy gifts and deafness to thy call, teaching us to sacrifice our comforts for others, making us kindly in thought, gentle in word, generous in deed.

O God, who hast taught us to pray for the coming of thy kingdom, strengthen all who are striving after true human relatedness and who are working for justice and peace. Restrain in us and in all people every temper which makes for war, all ungenerous judgments, all presumptuous claims, all promptings of self-assertion. Make us ready to recognize the needs and aspirations of other nations, and grant us the will to do what we can to remove misunderstanding and suspicion and to honor all people in Jesus Christ our Lord.

And now we pray for all who are sick in body or mind, for all who have lost relatives and friends, for all who are troubled by the suffering or sin of those they love, that in the dark and cloudy day they may find strength and peace in thee. Give us grace not to pass by suffering or joy without eyes to see. Give us sympathy and understanding. Use us to make others strong and happy and to shed forth thy light, which is the light of the world.

In the spirit of Christ we make our prayer. Amen.

—*Robert J. McCracken*

Eternal God, without whom life has no spiritual source, no divine meaning, purpose, or destiny, but with whom there is power for the present and hope for the future, we seek thee. So our ancestors before us have sought thee in their hour of need. Refresh our faith, that the strains of life may not break our spirits. Renew our courage, that life's dangers and disappointments may not intimidate our souls. Amid the tumult of these wild days, restore our confidence that this earth, like a ship, has a pilot, a compass, a course, and a haven. And if upon our lives such sorrow falls that happiness departs, grant us still a strong serenity, a secure trust, and a quiet peace.

Thanks be to thee for all the strength of character, the capacity for sacrifice, the courage, the forgetfulness of self, the loyalty even unto death, that in these tremendous days refresh our faith not only in thee but in the possibilities of humankind. O God, lay thy strong hand upon these noble qualities which we perversely use for the world's destruction, and turn them by thy grace to redeeming ends, to build a decent and peaceful earth.

Thanks be to thee for the rich heritage of our past, for our leaders, for the ideals of liberty and democracy, and for the manifold blessings of our country made sacred by the sacrifices of our ancestors. We pray for our country with full hearts and for our sons and daughters who represent it near and far.

For the world's sake, we pray for our churches, our homes, our schools, our leaders bearing their momentous responsibility, and for us the nation's citizens, that the power committed to our country, being wisely used, may lead us not through pride to desert thy purposes, but through humble obedience to thy will to peace and security and hope for all the world.

O God, who like the ocean art not only vast but near, as close to our souls as the lapping waters about the shores of an island, be near to us today. We need help. We are cast into strange places, met with heavy strains, burdened by poignant griefs. We are called on for tasks beyond our unaided strength, beset with temptations that defeat our weak resolves. We need cleansing and forgiveness, reinforcement and faith restored, that we may rise more than conquerors above the evils of the world, undaunted by its dangers and adequate for its opportunities. So meet our need today, and be to us our strength and hope and victory. We pray in the Spirit of Christ. Amen.

—*Harry Emerson Fosdick*

O God of our beautiful and burdened lives, we thank thee for the blessings of the week just past and pray that its hardships may strengthen us to live yet more creatively in the week ahead.

Give us faith, that we may take our defeats and turn them into occasions for the victories thou wouldst have us enjoy.

Give us faith, that in loneliness we may know thy company, and in distraction thy solitude.

Give us faith, that we who are Americans may accept the loss of our nation's power and not believe that it spells the end of the world, or even of us.

Give us faith, to leave in thy hands the well-being of those we love so dearly, especially those we now name before thee.

O God, we bless thee that thou wilt continue to be the hope of the dying, the friend of the poor, the leader of leaders, the succor of the tempted, the light of the wanderer, the joy of the pilgrim, the prosperity of thy church.

O great and merciful Creator, we pray in the name of our dear savior. Amen.   —*William Sloane Coffin Jr.*

O God, our Shepherd, your name comes easily to our lips because you have put yourself so fully into our hearts. So out of the fullness of our hearts, we, your not-too-often-enough-thankful children, come to worship you: to sing and rejoice and give thanks for your loving kindness, and for Jesus of Nazareth: our savior, our prize, our sustainer in all the vicissitudes of our restless lives.

What can we tell you today about ourselves, dear God, that you do not already know? Yet, in calling us friends, you ask us to pray to you—to pray without ceasing, with all kinds of prayer and supplication, to pray for all people everywhere, to pray with thanksgiving. Every act of prayer helps us keep believing that "I love therefore I am, I am honest therefore I am, I believe therefore I am." Every act of prayer reminds us that our lives have meaning beyond the natural and physical; that we are never alone; that help is always available; and that prayer changes things as well as people. Help us, your not-too-often-enough-believing children, to live knowing, "O what peace we often forfeit, O what needless pain we bear, all because we do not carry everything to God in prayer."

So, Blessed Creator, teach us to pray and save us from unwise praying. Let us not try to go it alone—we really cannot. Let us not secretly shred the stained files of our lives, trying to cover over our misdeeds—it will not work. Let us rather expose our lives, warts and all, to the camera of the cross, where forgiveness is abundantly provided and directions so lovingly given.

What can we tell you today about our world, dear God, that does not already grieve you? Heroes are made out of those who use sleight of hands, words, and truth; spectacle seems more important than substance; the temporary more prized than the permanent; duplicity propagated more than straightforwardness; and playing games with other people's lives more important than integrity, humility, justice, and peace.

What a challenge we have, as your not-too-often-enough-wise children, to live in this world but not be of this world; to be wounded with the wounded; to be homeless with the homeless; to hurt with the abused; to struggle with the addict; to feel prejudice with those who suffer such inhumanity; to see the potentials in all people; to fight alongside the peace mongers; to love the unloved; to give until it hurts; to feel this world's pain, as if it were our own assigned task to fix the whole messed up thing; and, alas, to laugh and rejoice with those who rejoice, and have fun with the one life you have given to us.

So, dear God, on this hot and sultry day in July in our city of New York, with eyes focused on things that really matter and with souls ready to march on in strength, we commit ourselves to you again, asking that through this service of worship we might see you more clearly, love you more dearly, and follow you more nearly, day by day. In the strong name of Christ, we pray. Amen.

—*Leo S. Thorne*

Gracious God, for nearly a century The Riverside Church has been a beacon on the hill called Morningside Heights, standing adjacent to, sharing community with, and learning from the great academic institutions that are its neighbors. Yet, in symbolism and substance, this church is called not only to be a student but also a teacher.

The stately tower adorning this edifice points minds to you, the ultimate source of all knowledge and wisdom. The majestic stained-glass windows are a kaleidoscope of color, calling people to appreciate the rainbow beauty of your creation. The magnificent organ sounds out harmonious notes of sisterhood and brotherhood that lift us beyond the cacophonous clamor of our divisive dogmas and provincial perspectives. The expansive nave represents the wideness in your mercy that is like the wideness of the sea.

Each element of the church's inspiring architecture teaches a lesson, but you have assigned this church a teaching task that extends beyond bricks and mortar. As we sit amid the halls of learning in this neighborhood and close to the center of capitalism on Wall Street, you call us to administer a moral examination that reveals whether the tenderness in our hearts matches the toughness of our minds. Ever remind The Riverside Church, O God, of its responsibility to raise this poignant question: How do we spell the word "prophet/profit?"

For this examination, no pens or papers, computers or classrooms are needed. We must simply ask people to write the answer on the tablets of their hearts. The letters used to spell "prophet/profit" indicate whether we have earned a degree in courage or whether we have instead majored in convenience and comfort. If profit is spelled in only a monetary way, then we may have academic training, but our moral education is woefully incomplete.

The market culture around us typically asks, "How can we make a *monetary* profit?" Merciful God, empower this church to ask instead, "Who is a *moral* prophet?" A profit may be a large monetary quantity, or a prophet may be a person with a large moral commitment. Careers that are economically profitable may be one kind of success, but lives that are courageously prophetic are what you ultimately desire.

In order to be faithful, prophets must not just accrue financial profits; we need heavenly insight that penetrates beneath the surface to expose the truth, the real truth, and nothing but the truth. Help us, O God, to really see. Help us to see how the heinous terrorist attacks of 2001 have been used to justify a narrow nationalism and a cult of militaristic revenge. Help us to see how the prison industrial complex has become the new plantation. Strange "fruit" no longer hangs from southern trees. Now the "fruit" simply spoils in steel containers called penitentiaries. Help us to see that so many lesbian, gay, bisexual, and transgender persons are suffering emotional and physical violence, while many religious communities remain eerily silent about the rights and dignity of our marginalized sisters and brothers. Clarify our prophetic insight by removing the cataracts of social complacency.

God of Miriam and Deborah, God of Isaiah and Jeremiah, raise up a new generation of moral prophets! Let a new generation of moral prophets save our nation from its petty red-state, blue-state divisions so that we all will fight poverty, the enemy with no party allegiance. Let a new generation of moral prophets teach us that the best "social security" consists in raising the income of the poor, improving public education, and providing affordable housing. Let a new generation of moral prophets exhort us to use public goods for the common good.

A long time ago, a wandering teacher from Galilee administered his own moral examination with the question, "What does it profit you to gain the whole world and lose your soul?" In a world greedy for monetary profits, let The Riverside Church faithfully make moral prophets—people willing to spend their lives in service to others and in praise of you. Amen.

—*Brad Braxton*

O God, thank you for sharing your divine life with us, that life which brought this world into being, that life which sustains this world, and that life which keeps us day-by-day. We have come to know that life through your Son, Jesus Christ, who has revealed your fullness to us. Such wondrous knowledge is too great for our minds to grasp. We can apprehend it only by faith. We marvel that we walk around this planet with sparks of divinity in us! With grateful hearts we say, "Thank you, God, for sharing yourself with us."

O Divine Spirit, there is nothing hid from you, not even our most secret desire. Our darkest thoughts shine like the noonday sun in your presence; our deepest cry is heard like the roaring thunder in your heart; and our weakest moment is reinforced like the waiting shores of the mighty ocean. So, as we enter your presence in prayer, teach us to be honest, if not with ourselves, with you, who know all things. Invade us by your spirit and capture our hearts afresh today, that we may settle for no less than your best for us. Dear God, remind us that there is so much more good stuff in us waiting to get out that we have not yet seen the half of what you can do in us and through us. So ignite our imagination this morning to dream a little more and not to settle for the harsh, distorted reality of a world which is yet to learn that God indeed exists.

And, God, we have a specific request today: Our church is at a crossroad, facing a real challenge to our future. On the one hand, we are in the dark, not quite knowing what to do, for change does not always forecast clear direction, and it is so easy to miss the right way when the light is not quite bright.

But on the other hand, we are not really without light. We have you, the divine light of our lives, and we know that this is your church. You have given us here, on the west side of this city, a group of terrific, bright, gifted people in this congregation, whose hearts strive to be in the right place. We hold your work in highest esteem, we love Riverside, and we want to do the right thing. We desire to choose, not the easy, comfortable road of status-quo Christianity and retreat from the front line. We chose to be placed in the thickest part of the battle in a world where injustice reigns and prejudices of all kinds abound. We see the rich growing inordinately richer, and the poor, hungry, needy, and homeless being sent empty away.

So, as we search ourselves first, dear God, and then we turn to intelligent work over the next couple of Sundays and the months ahead, let us be seduced by nothing less than your direction for our church. Let us recover the Spirit's mighty wind as you blow your fire among us. For after all, unless God builds the house, they labor in vain who build it. Remind us that as your church we do not have to fight *for* victory; we fight *from* victory already won by your divine Son, whose life is in us, here and now, and in whose name we pray. Amen.

— *Leo S. Thorne*

Special Days

Martin Luther King Jr.'s Birthday

We thank you, O God, that somehow in the midst of the confusion and disintegration of life you have spoken, as you often do, through one who was of the lineage and faith of an exploited people. So it is that at this time we remember Martin Luther King Jr., and as we do, we recall how strange it is that you often speak through those whom humankind has rejected. How strange—that from those who are the oppressed come the saviors not only of their own people but of all peoples everywhere. How profound and reassuring about the human spirit that those who are so markedly persecuted become the lovers of life, the peacemakers, and the instruments by which you establish human community and justice.

Martin King was a man who belonged to a race that has every reason to hate, and yet he preached by way of his actions an almost unbearable and seemingly ridiculous goodwill toward the enemy. When he spoke of creative goodwill—one that would suffer humiliation and ultimately change the heart of the oppressor, he dared risk the wrath, criticism, and disrespect of the society—and even his own people. But Martin King believed with all his heart that you, God, the Creator of life, the Integrating Spirit that ties all life together, have revealed yourself in the flesh and blood of Jesus. And if one were going to walk the way that Jesus walked, one must be willing to take the road that leads to Calvary. Amen.   —*George Thomas*

O God of Love, Power, and Justice, who wills the freedom and fulfillment of all your children. We thank you for the constancy of your loving kindness and tender mercies toward us. Especially on this day as we celebrate the birthday and life of your servant and prophet, Dr. Martin Luther King Jr. We are reminded that in every age you raise up seers and sayers and doers of justice. We marvel at the way by which you shaped a young black boy from Georgia into a towering figure of his time—to awaken the conscience of the nations, to rekindle a passion for freedom, equality, and peace; to redirect the traffic of human affairs from the back alley of bigotry toward the grand concourse of courage and compassion. We stand in awe at the marvelous networking by which you built a movement around a man of vision. It included blacks and whites; Protestants, Catholics, and Jews; conservatives and progressives; rich and poor; business and labor. This "coalition of conscience" dedicated itself to the proposition that the American dream of freedom and equality could be made real through courageous action in a spirit of love, in pursuit of human dignity for all. This dignity includes all who suffer from homelessness, joblessness, purposelessness, carelessness, hopelessness.

Because our needs are so great today, and your care so constant, we know that you are rebuilding the network of compassion around new visionaries whom you have assembled for this hour. Surprise us with the discovery of how much power we have to make a difference in our day:

A difference in the way citizens meet, greet, respect, and protect the rights of each other.

A difference in the breadth of our vision of what is possible in humanization, reconciliation, and equalization of results in our great city.

A difference in the way government, business, and labor can work together, for justice and social enrichment.

A difference in our response to the needy, and a difference
in our appreciation for those who give of themselves for
the surviving and thriving of our beautiful people.

Use this season of celebration to spark new hope and stir up
our passion for new possibilities. Make compassion and the
spirit of sacrifice to be the new mark of affluence of character. Strengthen us to face reality and to withstand the rigor of
tough times in the anticipation of a bright side beyond the
struggle. Inspire, empower, and sustain us until we reach the
mountaintop and see that future for which our hearts yearn.

This is our fervent and sincere prayer. Amen.

—*James Forbes Jr.*

Bountiful God, we are so very grateful that you have created
new hearts in us and bounded the world through laws of justice. We are gathered today in need of your help.

We ask your loving presence for those in our lives who
have special needs, in illness, grief, and joy. O God of Wisdom,
for all the moments of joy, in the laughter of little children, in
the deep radiance of sunrise, and in intimate moments with
others, we have trouble in our world. We need to be close to
your child Jesus, for our way is steep, and we have heart and
vision problems. We are often so overwhelmed with work,
pain, and loneliness; our hearts are troubled and numbed.
We are often so confused by the mix and speed of our time;
our inner eye of spirit cries out for clarity and the assurance of
your hope. We know—we know, Lord, you accept in us what
we cannot know, you name in us what we cannot say, and you
hold in your memory what we have tried to forget. All these
things in our ignorance we cannot *yet* confess.

On this first day of the week, in resurrection faith, we
gather to remember our world's minister, Martin Luther King

Jr., who risked his life to proclaim that we are *all* yours. Dr. King lost his life because *that* truth is too powerful for the powerful to endure. For Jesus' sake, and in Dr. King's honor, God, make us tough channels of your peace. Help us to own up to hatreds within and without ourselves that hurt, divide, and destroy; to own up to injury in mind, body, and spirit that renders us without direction; and to own up to despair that we do not know how to be just with each other in little things, while we turn away impoverished from the important, big things.

O God of Abraham and Sarah, of Christ and Mary, you know well that your work for a just peace that shook the foundations of the earth through Dr. King *is not done.* Help us continue his work. We need clarity to heal our ignorance. We need courage to heal our despair. We need his righteous boldness to dream *together* for the life of freedom. Give us the gift of memory, God, to remember the other Martin Luther who risked for truth when he said, "Here I stand, I can do no other." In our time, Dr. King spoke truth to power and took the lonely walk into the unknown, risking abandonment by the church, the government, and his friends. Yet in his lonely resolve, he said, "I will be where I have always been, in the hands of Almighty God." Teach us to live in the power of those words of confident faith!

We can and do confess, God, that we have *more to learn* from these disciples named Martin in the Communion of Saints. May we stand strong in such faith as theirs in the name of Jesus. Amen. —*Fanny Erickson*

Abraham Lincoln's Birthday
St. Valentine's Day

We rejoice in the events of the coming week: the birthday of Abraham Lincoln, the spiritual center of our history; the fun of St. Valentine's Day.

We pray thee to move us, the American people, closer to our center. Free us, O God, from the fear that corrupts our wisdom for the sake of power; from the fear that trivializes, that divides us as a people, especially rich from poor; from the fear that prompts us to make authority our truth instead of truth our authority. And we pray for the church, that it may be courageous and compassionate in times that are sure to be uncertain.

Guide, O most merciful Creator, the thinking of rulers the world around. May they not confuse violence with strength or compassion with weakness. May they not use the imperfections of international relations as an excuse to perpetuate them; rather, may they see that the high purpose of rulers is to keep hope advancing, to straighten out this tangled world, to make people good—by their own choosing. With malice toward none and charity to all, may we all press forward until we can say of this world what we can gratefully say of this day, "Beautiful, beyond any singing of it." Amen.

—*William Sloane Coffin Jr.*

George Washington's Birthday

Eternal God, who hast made us so that our hearts are restless until they rest in thee, we make our approach to thee in hope and expectation. In this house of praise and prayer we have often heard thy voice and seen thy glory. Here we have found release from the tension of life. Here our fears and forebodings have vanished. Here the deepest cravings of our natures have been satisfied. Renew to us these mercies. Grant us now a vivid sense of thy nearness. Fill our hearts with joy and our lips with song.

Forgive us, we beseech thee, for our sins. We are not what we ought to be. We have done things which we ought not to have done; we have left undone things which we ought to have done; there are times when, despairingly, we wonder whether there is any health in us. Pardon our offenses, O God—our selfishness, our thoughtlessness, our persistent neglect of thee. So change our hearts and renew our wills that we shall love that which thou dost love and do that which thou dost command, and with singleness of mind and purpose seek first thy kingdom and thy righteousness.

O gracious God, who hast cast our lot in pleasant places, we praise thee for our goodly heritage in this land. We remember with gratitude those whose gifts of head and heart and hand established the foundations of this nation. We bless thee for the ideals of faith and freedom which they cherished.

Help us to hold them dear and to prize them above luxury or ease. Deliver us from pride and self-sufficiency. In prosperity, let us not forget thee; in the hour of achievement let us not be unmindful of our dependence on thee. Grant to our leaders purity of motive, soundness of judgment, the faith of their forebears, and to all our people fidelity, integrity, and real religion, that there may be peace and prosperity within our borders and that we may be an influence for righteousness throughout the world.

Raise up in every land leaders of vision and courage who for the sake of the common good will think wisely and do justly and love mercy. Let goodwill reign in the hearts of all humankind, and bring us speedily out of our present confusion into the order and righteousness of thy kingdom; through him who is the Prince of Peace and the Savior of the world, in whose spirit and name we pray. Amen.   —*Robert J. McCracken*

Festival of the Christian Home

On this special day, let us pray for all who, young and old, belong to each other and go through life together. Let us pray that we may care for and respect each other, that we may not be divided, but may with one mind try to achieve happiness.

Let us pray for a happy childhood for all children and for all who are defenseless and small: that nothing may harm them; that their lives may not become distorted and perverse; that we may not teach them to hate, but rather lead them to truth.

Let us pray for our young people, whose lives lie ahead of them: that they may go forward with receptive minds to meet their future; that they may learn to live with life's uncertainties and face up to disappointments; that they may learn to accept themselves and not lose heart.

Let us pray for all who are in the prime of life: that they may be fruitful; that they may not be self-seeking, but rather seek the welfare of others.

Let us pray for all adults, whether married or single: that they may not be lonely, complacent, or closed to others, but that they may go on seeking others' friendship and thus grow in humanity.

Let us pray for all middle-aged people: that they may stay young in heart; that they may have wisdom and openness, may not be conservative or envious, but might allow latitude to young people.

Let us pray for the aged: that they may not be left behind in life, but still put their experience to good use in the service of others and be treated with respect and affection.

Let us pray for those who are troubled with illness, for all who are anxious and afraid of death: that they may be given light and faith, a spirit of surrender and peace.

Let us pray also for those who cannot find satisfaction, those who have failed in work or in life: that they might place their hopes in the future and not lose faith in God, who does not want us to be lost.

Let us pray for ourselves: that young and old we may constantly be made new people by God's grace; that we may banish from our midst all discord and mistrust; that we do not break with each other, though we may be separated by age; that God may keep us together as father and daughter, as mother and son, as one family and one people the world around. Amen.

—*William Sloane Coffin Jr.*

Harry Emerson Fosdick's Birthday

Almighty God, Creator of the world in which we live and Builder of the church through which we serve, it is good and altogether right, whatever our mood or station, that we should praise thy name.

We thank thee for words of encouragement that find us when our flame is low;
> for helpful hands that reach us when the load is more than we can bear;
> for retrievable insights that come to mind when two ways open and we must decide.
> Nor would we fail to thank thee for thy governance and love,
> and for all who by word and life and dependence on thy Spirit have brought our doubting souls to faith.

We remember with gratitude the founding pastor of this church,
> the scope of his agile mind,
> the vision that commanded him,
> and the lives he touched across the years of a long and fruitful life.

Help us to continue what he so well began, and to thy name be praise.
> Through Jesus Christ our Lord. Amen.

—*Ernest T. Campbell*

Memorial Day

Gracious God, whose own Son's term of service to humanity was so full that its brevity was no distress, we call to mind on this Memorial Sunday those "who will not grow old as we who are left grow old," those whose lives were too brief for us but long enough, perhaps, for thee. Forgive us that they died so young because we were too unimaginative, too imperious, too indifferent, or just too late to think of better ways than warfare to conduct the business of the world. Gratefully we remember the generosity that prompted them to share the last of their rations, the last pair of dry socks, to share in the course of one hour in a foxhole more than most of us care to share with another in a lifetime. And we recall the courage that made more than one of them fall on the grenade there was no time to throw back.

Grant, O God, that they may not have died in vain. May we draw new vigor from past tragedy. Buttress our instincts for peace, sorely beleaguered. Save us from justifications invented to make us look noble, grand, and righteous and from blanket solutions to messy, detailed problems. Give us the vision to see that those nations that gave the most to their generals and least to their poor were, throughout all history, the first to fall. Most of all, give us the vision to see that the world is now too dangerous for anything but truth, too small for anything but love. Through Jesus Christ our Lord, who became what we are to make us what he is. Amen.   —*William Sloane Coffin Jr.*

Independence Day

O God, mightily we pray for wisdom, courage, and strength to serve thee and this nation faithfully in the days that lie ahead. Remind us of our duty to promote the general welfare, to secure the blessings of liberty for all, to see to it that justice and compassion reign from sea to shining sea, and that the bountiful resources of a favored land are not only thankfully received but also gladly shared with the whole human family.

We know, O God, that this vision of America has never been fully realized, but it has never been abandoned. Remind us that it has been significant to the rest of the world, where echoes and adaptations of it are seen in the revolutions and the constitutions of many nations; it has been a magnet to our own people, charming them away from slavery and sweatshops, chain gangs and lynch mobs, toward broader opportunity, deeper compassion, fuller equality, and greater justice for all. O God, grant wisdom and courage for the living of these days.

Hear too our prayer for those in this congregation and the globe around who are in trouble, sorrow, need, sickness, or any other adversity; may they feel thine everlasting arms. O God, bless this congregation. Bless our worship here today. May thy Holy Spirit be like penetrating oil to loosen the rusted hinges of our hearts, so that we swing wide the doors to thee and to one another. Amen.   —*William Sloane Coffin Jr.*

Arab Spring

O God, our refuge and our strength, watch over us today! Watch over our tumultuous world in these weeks filled with revolutionary hope, sacrifice, and danger. Guide us all as we approach this turning point in our world and in our nation. Guide our feet, God, while we run this race. For we do not want to run this race in vain.

As we see our world torn apart and watch the courageous crowds in Libya and Egypt, in Tunisia and Bahrain, in Jordan and Yemen, with others waiting to join the throngs, we see a vast tide of irrepressible human longing breaking down the dams of oppressive and ruthless regimes. When we listen to the voices of the afflicted and forgotten, we hear your voice,

O God, speaking through the universal human hunger for freedom, justice, and hope. We see your spirit in the daring courage required to topple the pharaohs of bondage and corruption. You are the God who sees pain, brutality, and oppression and reaches with outstretched hand into the hearts of your people.

O God, help us, in these times, to confront our own institutional pharaohs; our own unrestrained predators; our own widening gap between the indulgences of super wealthy people and the abandoned needs of middle-class and poor people. Guide our feet, God, lest we lose our way and become a nation ruled by the rich for the rich. Help us find the courage and moral resources to rebuild our nation into a place of hope for all its citizens, wealthy and poor! Help us to reclaim a vision of justice that includes all of us. Help us to ensure that no one is excluded from housing and healthcare or education and opportunity. Help us to understand that if we tolerate inequality, poverty, and racism, we will always have violence in our midst. For poverty is violent. Exploitation is violent. Homelessness is violent. These are forms of violence that violate all of us and can turn the American Dream into the American Lie. In these challenging times, O God, show us the way and guide our feet! Give us the courage to turn our nation and your world into a place of hope for every child, every woman, every human being created in your divine image. For we are our brother and our sister.

Help us all ride through the storms of these times, centered and grounded in your love for all of us. Help us to remain calm, as if we are at the hub of a wheel that is gradually turning in the right direction. Help us to remember that suffering is not an individual matter—it requires all of us to pull together, guided and strengthened by your love. Grant us wisdom, courage, and hope for the living of these days. Amen.   —*Joan Kavanaugh*

Labor Day

Eternal God, high above all yet deep within us all, far off so that the stars are in thy leash, and yet the flame of spiritual life in everyone, we pause once more amid the rush of busy life to stand in awe and reverence before the thought of thee.

We come before thee because we have minds and must use them. We live in the midst of mystery inexplicable, its deeps too profound for our plummets, its towering facts too high for us to see their cloudy peaks. Yet we cannot believe the mystery has no explanation. We dare not think that it is a sea without a bottom, a process without a meaning, a universe without purpose and destiny. Only when we come to thee and find in thee the creative Power that is behind all, the meaning running through all, and the goal ahead, do our thoughts find rest. We would love thee this day, O God, with all our minds.

We come to thee because we are workers. We care about great enterprises on the earth. We are concerned for our homes and our churches, our nation, and the world's peace. We give our lives to tasks in which we verily believe. We dare not think that they mean nothing and will issue nowhere. In hope we must be saved, and only when we turn to thee, O thou who art able to keep that which we commit unto thee against that day, only when we stand before thee and cry like thy Son, "My Father worketh hitherto, and I work," do we find strength and courage, confidence and power in our labor.

We come to thee, O God, because we are sinners. Sinners we confess ourselves, tempted repeatedly by prizes that evil promises but cannot give and, deceived for years, willing still to be fooled once more. How often have we been led by sin into the wilderness and left there; yet we have followed sin again! We need forgiveness and we need power. Of our own strength we are not sufficient. We return evermore to thee,

O thou who canst strengthen us with power by thy Spirit in our inner selves.

We come to thee, O God, because we are sufferers. Hardship has dug its plowshares deep into the souls of some of us. We have been beaten and crushed and broken on the wheel of life. Health has gone. Bereavement has opened wide its awful misery. Estate has been broken, O God in the heights, canst thou understand thy children who still must carry their crosses up their Calvary? We need strength to understand and to endure—confident amid all untoward experiences that at the heart of all there is purpose and goodwill. We need power, not simply to bear but to use the tragedy, to build it into stronger character and to come off more than conquerors. Because else we are undone with dismay or embittered with rebellion we come to thee, O thou God of all comfort.

We come to thee, O God, because we are lovers. Friendship binds us one to another's heart and makes life very beautiful. We rejoice before thee in our friendships and our families. We should be bereft if we thought that love was but an accident and did not reveal something deep in thy heart. O God, thou art love. Our lips would learn to say it once again, because we are lovers. We come to thee because we are mortals and our little life is rounded with a sleep. We come to an end as a tale that is told. We cannot by anxious thought add a cubit to our stature or a day to our years when the end has come. Yet we do not believe that our mortality is the story's end. This corruptible must put on incorruption, and this mortal must put on immortality. O thou whom to know aright is life eternal, we children of an earthly day and a heavenly hope worship thee.

Thou seest how our needs gather themselves together in thee: our minds, our work, our sins, our sufferings, our loves, and our mortality. As thus we seek thee because of our deep needs, we pray for all kindred souls around the world of every name or sign who open themselves receptively to the resources of the divine Spirit this day. We all are very fallible in our thoughts of thee. We all fall short of adequacy in our imaginations of thy meaning. Yet thou dost circumvent the barricades we build against thee. Thou dost rise above the insufficiency of our imagination of thee. So do thou this day around the world wherever people seek thee, flood in upon them with thy righteousness and power and peace. Lift all our life to higher levels. Give us more sympathy, more generosity, more magnanimity! Give us more holy indignation against things evil. Give us deep and moving love for things that are wholesome, saving, and excellent, so that righteousness and peace may kiss each other on this earth. In the name of Christ, who loved us and gave himself for us. Amen.

—Harry Emerson Fosdick

Our God, our Help in Ages Past, and our Eternal Home, we come to you with gratitude for the capacity to work, to create, and to care. Yet, we come with troubled spirits, for we are vulnerable and fearful of change, and we share so much pain with other beings on this planet.

On this Labor Day, we celebrate your creation, the work of your fingers. We are blessed that you have created us to be workers, God, just like you. Yet our work is part of our troubles: often we work without affirmation; often we do our work in ways not pleasing to you; and sometimes we impose our wills on others and make their work lives hard and alienated. Some of us still try to work with joy, and some of us work as captive birds in gilded cages.

When we see others' work and buy their products, we try not to think about where things are made, who made them, how old the workers are, how much they are paid, or how safe their working conditions are. It is so easy to turn our heads away from the larger universe of work and hold our breath when working hours are limited so as not to pay benefits; when cruel conditions are created to make us leave our jobs; when a few are richly rewarded to live in affluence and the many go away with paychecks that barely provide what they need.

On Labor Day, when our society seems unable to assure most of us with the stability of lifelong employment, of care when we are weak, and of respect when we grow old, we lift our hearts to you, our hope, that we may be born again into the goodness of the Living Christ. We would work together with your Spirit for a just peace, to bring the global change that could meet the common needs of our being human together, to create a world where all workers share in the abundance you have made available to us. Only by challenging the powers of this world can we bow before Jesus as Sovereign God, who lived the gospel in which the powerful and rich were brought down and the poor and weak lifted up.

We pray for the world you have given us, that you would be with those who are peacemakers, those who are in danger in war, those combat veterans still recovering from their injury to mind and body, and those who have lost hope of living ordinary life ever again.

O God, who is still working to create a new thing, breathe into us now the strength of rock solidness that Jesus saw in Peter, so that we may build the ministries of a just peace in the spirit of Jesus Christ, the Light of the world. Amen.

—*Fanny Erickson*

Laity Sunday

We remember before thee today the lay people of thy church whose witness to thee is largely made beyond these walls. We thank thee,

for Christian teachers, Christian lawyers, and Christian
  businesspeople;

for Christians in politics, Christians in building construc-
  tion and maintenance, Christians in the arts,

for Christians in the home.

Bless them with a sense of thy presence on the job, to the end
that they may do their work well and in the doing of it be a
Christ to those around them.

Forgive us that our influence has never matched our
numbers:

  that we have spent more time enjoying our faith than apply-
    ing it;

  that so many of our friends have no idea at all of what Christ
    means to us.

  Where others drift, help us to move with purpose.

  Where others doubt, help us to believe.

  Where others despair, help us to hope in thee.

  Through Jesus Christ our Lord.

O thou searcher of all hearts, in whose sight the fine print of
our private history is as a billboard, whatever else we may lack
in our worship, let us at least be as honest as we can.

  Deliver us from the need to build ourselves up by cutting
    others down.

  Free us from the pride that makes acknowledgment of wrong
    difficult.

  Give us the grace to back away from earlier positions with
    the coming of fresh light.

  Keep us at peace in the center of our being, however turbu-
    lent the causes we support.

  Let thy comfort enfold every grieving heart among us.

May the stout promises of thy Holy Word embolden all who
   are afraid,
And thy judgments shake the lethargy of all who are at ease
   in Zion.
Through Jesus Christ our Lord. Amen.

—Ernest T. Campbell

Peace Sabbath

O God, who hast created a world beautiful beyond any singing of it, gratefully we acknowledge that of thy fullness have we
received grace upon grace. Grant now that we may be respon-
sible in the measure that we have received.

Keep us eager to pursue truth beyond the outermost limits of human thought, scornful of the cowardice that dares not
face new truth, the laziness content with half-truth, and the
arrogance that thinks it knows all truth.

Strengthen our resolve to see fulfilled, the world around
and in our time, all hopes for justice so long deferred, and
keep us on the stony, long, and lonely road that leads to
peace. May we think for peace, struggle for peace, suffer for
peace. Fill our hearts with courage, that we not give in to bitterness and self-pity but learn rather to count pain and disappointment, humiliation and setback, as but straws on the
tide of life.

So may we run and not grow weary, walk and not faint,
until that day when, by thy grace, faith and hope will be out-
distanced by sight and possession, and love will be all in all in
this wonderful, terrible, beautiful world. Amen.

—William Sloane Coffin Jr.

A Litany for Peace

(This litany was used at the service of worship in The Riverside Church on behalf of a new world order in view of the United Nations Conference in San Francisco in 1945.)

Unison: Eternal God, Creator of all humankind, we bow before thee in humility and in hope. Thy ways have not been our ways, neither have thy thoughts been our thoughts. Yet thou hast not forsaken us, though we have passed through the fires of suffering and dwelt in the valley of sorrow. In thy mercy grant us thy light and thy truth; let them lead us from the road of destruction toward the city of life and peace. So fashion our desires and deeds in accordance with thy will, that we may yet build the new world of righteousness for which thy Son was willing to die and for which so many people are now offering their lives.

Minister: O God, who art the hope of the ends of the earth, hear us while we pray: that it may please thee to bless with wisdom, mutual respect, and confidence, and with a desire for the common good, the representatives of the United Nations who have this day assembled; to endow them with a right understanding and a pure purpose, and to enable them to rise above national self-interest into the larger thoughts of world peace and human unity.

People: We beseech thee to hear us, O God, as we pray...

Minister: That it may please thee: to save us from pride of possession and of power, from vainglorious boasting, from neglect of opportunity and evasion of responsibility, from failure to consider the needs of others because we desire to live to ourselves alone, from trusting in our own strength when the world's salvation rests on the observance of thy will, from saying what we do not mean and from striving after what we should not have.

People: We beseech thee to hear us, O God , as we pray. . .

Minister: That it may please thee to bless thy church universal with faith and courage and a steadfast heart, that desiring unity among the nations it may obtain unity within itself; that the real enemies of humankind—ignorance, poverty, disease, and all other evils—may be known and overcome; that the life-giving Spirit of Jesus may never languish, and that the vision of the kingdom of God may never grow dim.

People: We beseech thee to hear us, O God , as we pray. . .

Minister: That it may please thee to grant us hope which will rise above frustration; patience which will endure the strain of waiting; goodwill which cannot be offended; forgiveness for all who have made their peace with thee; and trust in thy providence, which can use even the wrath of humanity to praise thee.

People: We beseech thee to hear us, O God.

Unison: Eternal God, who art our refuge and strength, we commit ourselves to thee. Dedicate us afresh to our unfinished task, that we may win the peace for which good people have died. Hasten through us the day when all of us shall dwell in safety among our neighbors, free from want, free from fear, free to speak our thoughts, and free to worship according to the guidance of thy Spirit; and thine shall be the kingdom and the power and the glory forever. Amen.

September 16, 2001
(after the terrorist attack on 9/11)

Eternal God—Shepherd, Redeemer, and Savior—this morning we need you, and we need each other. Let us join in a moment of silence and solidarity with all who have died and with all who love them, for our hearts are with them. O God of Life, today we return to you from a wasteland of terror, violence, and cruelty. We come as refugees, lost and stunned. We come thirsty and hungry for you. We come with fear for our future and for our children. We come feeling vulnerable, our safety shattered along with our towers of economic and military strength. We come from a world torn apart by rising fanaticism, intolerance, and injustice. We come in frustration and anger, and in deep, deep sadness.

And yet, even through the unspeakable horror of this week, you have clearly been with us. We have seen your presence in the heroism and courage of rescuers who risked their own lives for strangers. We have seen your face in the exhausted faces of firefighters and police officers, in rescue workers who toiled beyond exhaustion to find survivors. We have seen your love in the rivers of generosity and compassion that poured through thousands of volunteers who went to help with gifts of medical aid and blood; with food, socks, and prayers.

This week, we have seen with our own eyes that you are with us in the valley of the shadow of death, even in the presence of our enemies. We have seen you in the power of our deepened sense of connection with each other, transcending all that we ever, in pettier moments, allowed to divide us. It has been a dark week, with winds of evil blowing that we have smelled in the very air around us. And now we turn to you to be that light, that inextinguishable light that will overcome this darkness of ours. In these desperate times, when the world is endangered and hope seems small, when the tides of revenge are running high, we need your light and wisdom to show us the way forward.

You are not the God of hate we have seen worshiped this week. You are the God of Life! And as our nation strategizes its response, we must all remember that you place before us life and death, and ask us always to choose *life*. Teach us and our world community what this means. Teach us, before it is too late, that violence begets violence and that these new forms of warfare have no victors. Teach us that we are perpetrators of violence, as well as its victims, that we cannot isolate ourselves from suffering in this world or live in relative luxury for ourselves alone. Teach us that fanatics and terrorists are born in camps of suffering, injustice, and poverty. Teach us that religious fanaticism of all persuasions always has and always will have a high body count. Teach us that hatred ceases not when it is met with hatred, but when it is met with justice and compassion.

If we really want to root out terrorists, we must not merely go to their cells and training camps, but also to the conditions of human injustice and dogmatic arrogance that breed terrorism in the first place.

Teach us to be wary of turning our enemies into Satan, lest we find that we are infected with the same cancer. Teach us to demonize no country or religion, for God, you speak to all of us, not in English, Arabic, or Hebrew, but in the universal language of human suffering. Teach our world leaders to listen to the voices of suffering if they want to build a coalition for a peaceful and secure world. Teach us to be moderate and wise. Teach us that love is our most efficient and, perhaps, only means of survival.

O God of Love and Life, thy will be done, thy dominion come. Give us sufficient light to see your will. Re-enter our lives that we might put goodness, not vengeance, at the center. Center our lives around faith, not fear. When our strength wanes, help us to rely upon yours. For in the power of your love, we are afflicted but not crushed, persecuted but not forsaken, struck down but not destroyed. Your love will heal our broken places and make us whole again.

We pray for the healing of the whole world, including our enemies. Make us all instruments of lasting peace. Amen.

—Joan Kavanaugh

Reformation Sunday

O God our Creator, we pray for thy church, and specifically for this church: may it be free, courageous, and compassionate, not fearful or rigid; a safe harbor when the winds of the world are high against us, and the only safe ship in which to sail out of the harbor to take on the storms of life.

We thank thee for the history of the church, a past that inspires our hearts with the dedication of the saints and martyrs. Ordained to unrest, they dreamed visions larger than their times. Grant that we too in perilous days may not fear to engage in a lover's quarrel with our times.

O Jesus Christ, who bleeding and broken and bowed, yet still unconquered, dost reign from the cross, pour out thy Spirit on all thy churches. Revive thy work. Raise up laborers, O Lord, that men and women may be ready to tell of thy justice and peace and of thy salvation unto the ends of the earth. Amen.

—William Sloane Coffin Jr.

All Saints' Day

O God, we gather once more to acknowledge that the good things of this world still outweigh the bad, that we can, therefore, live gratefully, not dutifully; joyfully, not with grim determination.

We thank thee for this our church, and we remember especially today the rare and radiant people of its past who gave voice and life to its best aspirations. May we, who follow, not forget the lessons they taught: that where there is doubt there is more considered faith; that self-pity and bitterness are diminishing emotions; and that the price of hating others is to love oneself less.

Grant, O God, that we may be loyal to their memory by furthering their highest hopes. In the spirit of Jesus Christ we pray. Amen.   —*William Sloane Coffin Jr.*

Election Day

O God, who hast created this world of tender beauty which now is laden with such fragile hopes, gratefully we acknowledge that no morning stars that sing together have deeper cause than we for joy, for of thy fullness have we received grace upon grace.

For blue days filled with rushing clouds, for parks and rivers and neighbors and friends, for the knowledge that there are no more important tragedies than the tragedy of death and no more important victories than the victory of love, God, we praise thy holy name.

And we thank thee for the light streaming from the cross, which discloses not the reasons for pain and injustice (for they remain a mystery), but discloses thee suffering with and for us and by that suffering bringing light and life. O God, that what we know makes bearable what we do not know, that in all ages and lands dark valleys have been turned into havens of light, crosses into shrines, God, for all this we bless thy holy name.

O God, gross darkness now covers the earth and thy people. Come then to thy children, not only as light but also as a consuming fire to set ablaze all the rubbish of the earth: the chauvinism of the nations, the obsolete barriers that sunder those who should be seeing eye to eye and working side by side, the banality of so much of our culture, and the shells and husks, the remnants of our unconsecrated selves. Make us, O God, faithful Christians not only in Galilee but also in Jerusalem. May we seek not to limit the liabilities of our witness, but rather to be loyal and loving to thee and to our neighbors, O loving and faithful Creator of us all. Amen.

—*William Sloane Coffin Jr.*

Thanksgiving Day

Eternal God, high and lifted up and yet within us all, with dutiful and adoring awe we come to worship thee. We, who through another week have too much looked down on things beneath, would turn our eyes to things above. We, who too often have contented ourselves with the things that serve us, would now look to the things that have a right to command us. We would be carried out of ourselves by something greater than ourselves to which we give ourselves.

Lift us up, we beseech thee, into the spirit of adoration. Help us to see in life whatever is excellent and beautiful, august and of good report, that we may be no longer disillusioned and dismayed before the ugliness of life but may renew our confidence in God and godliness.

Lift us up into the spirit of thanksgiving. Quicken our sense of gratitude. If in the unending conversation within our minds we have spoken to ourselves only about our difficulties and our ills, help us to remember this day the benedictions that have made life beautiful and the blessings through which thou hast shined upon us. Recall to our thought our friends, the homes that have nourished us, the people who have loved us, great books, great music, great art, those who in sacrifice laid the foundations of the social securities which we enjoy. Make real to us him who loved us and gave himself for us, and so elevate our worship, we beseech thee, until it is a festival. Help us to celebrate our God this day in the spirit of thanksgiving.

Lift us up, we beseech thee, into the spirit of confession. Forgive us for the carelessness with which we regard those sins that hurt, not ourselves alone, but other lives as well. Teach us afresh that we cannot sin unto ourselves but that every evil grudge we harbor and every vindictive wish we cherish and every unkind, unclean thing we do is like poison given to our friends. Deepen within us, therefore, we beseech thee, our conscientiousness. Help us this day, with a fine sense of honor, honestly to face our own souls and to say before thee and one another, We have sinned.

Lift us up, we beseech thee, into the spirit of intercession. Save us from the narrowness of our sympathies. Keep us, we beseech thee, from our provinciality. Widen the borders of our understanding and our care. If we are prosperous, bring to our hearts the thought of the poor; if we are well, the sick; if we are happy, the sorrowful; if our family circles are unbroken, the bereaved; and help us in such sincerity to pray that we may go out to work and make our hearts and hands a channel through which the care of God can flow down into some unhappy life.

Lift us up, we beseech thee, to a higher thought about our country. In these feverish days, save us from being feverish. Give this country, we beseech thee, a finer spirit, a saner wisdom, and increased goodwill. Forbid us from our bigotry and our intolerance. Give us the grace of strong convictions joined with a sympathetic understanding of those who differ from us. Let wisdom be deepened in our commonwealth, that the great business which as a nation we have on hand may be wrought out in soberness and truth as becomes the children of our forebears.

Lift up our spirit into intercession for the church. Forgive it for its infidelity to its Lord. Forgive us the contrast between Christianity and Christ. He is so great; we are so unworthy. Upon all thy people everywhere, who in sincerity and truth, working in the spirit of Jesus, are lifting the levels of our human

life closer to oneness, righteousness, and peace, let thy benediction fall! Across the barriers that we have made, the sectarian lines that we have named, we pray unto the God who has
said, "All souls are mine." Save us from our narrowness into thy
breadth. Save us from our littleness to thy universality. O God,
who art great, make us great also in our love.

And now, beyond the power of our small words to carry the
needs of thy people here, do thou cross the inner thresholds
of our hearts and minister not according to our desert but
according to the riches of thy grace in Christ Jesus, our Lord.
Amen.   —*Harry Emerson Fosdick*

Gracious God, as the rising and setting of the sun bring different seasons in the heavens, so, too, there are different seasons on the horizon of our souls. Whether it is January or July,
Advent or Easter, the calendars hanging in our hearts do not
always match the calendars hanging on our walls. Since you,
Eternal One, are from everlasting to everlasting, your mercy
meets us and your grace goes with us in whatever season we
find ourselves.

If it is fall in our souls, you are still God, and we are still
thankful! Although we, like leaves, sit upon the tallest tree at
summer solstice, we plunge to the ground by autumn moon.
Thus, we fear the fall. In spite of their splendid colors, falling
leaves call us to remember our earthiness. Banish, O God, our
fear of the fall. May our fallen leaves send fresh nourishment
into the soil of our souls. The fall also is a time of pruning. Let
us remove dead branches in hope of new life, by and by. At the
tree in Eden, we fell from grace. Help us this time, dear God, to
fall *into* grace.

If it is winter in our souls, you are still God, and we are still
thankful! "As rain turns to snow, puddles to ice, the sun rises

later and sets earlier; and each day it climbs less high in the sky."[1] When winter's chill envelops us, and darkness descends upon us, our faith will not falter. Why should it falter, since you, O God, are the creator of darkness, as well as light? "God called the light Day and the darkness God called Night. And there was evening and there was morning, the first day" (Gen. 1:5 NRSV). On that morning of mornings in creation's dawning, before there was light, there was darkness—rich, ebony darkness; womb-like, winter darkness. Lord of the Shadows, do not deliver us from dimness, but dwell with us in dimness. Lead us into the luminous darkness, for the deeper we plunge into darkness, the more we comprehend the light.[2]

If it is spring in our souls, you are still God, and we are still thankful! "Winter returns a thousand times. But so does spring."[3] In newness of life, we welcome spring from its long winter break. Since last spring's gentle embrace, branches have been pruned and roots of faith have run deep into the soil. At long last, we are ready, really ready, for grace to germinate and blessings to blossom. "For now the winter is past. . . . The flowers appear on the earth; the time of singing has come" (Song of Solomon 2:11–12 NRSV). We sing in the emerging rays of the sun. We shout, "Hallelujah!" in the emerging rays of the Son, the Child of God. Clouds of doubt and dismay can never eclipse this sun. The Son—the Child of God—will never be hid! Spring up! The sun has risen! Spring up! Jesus has risen indeed!

If it is summer in our souls, you are still God, and we are still thankful! "Summer is the season when all the promissory

---

1. Madeleine L'Engle with Carole F. Chase, *Glimpses of Grace: Daily Thoughts and Reflections* (New York: Harper Collins, 1998), 3.

2. Inspired by Howard Thurman, *The Luminous Darkness* (Richmond, Ind.: Friends United Press, 1989).

3. Renita J. Weems, *Listening for God: A Minister's Journey through Silence and Doubt* (New York: Touchstone, 1999), 37.

notes of autumn, winter, and spring come due.[4] It is summer, and we no longer simply stand on your promises; we bask in your blessings, your abundant blessings, your radiant blessings; balmy summer blessings that warm the landscape of our lives; balmy summer breezes that unleash the sweet fragrance of the sweet fruit of the Spirit: "love, joy, peace, patience, kindness, generosity, faithfulness, gentleness, and self-control" (Gal. 5:22-23 NRSV). It is summer—a time not only for enjoying the harvest, but also for being the harvest in the lives of others. Some loveless relationship, some joyless child, some war-ripped nation needs our fruit of the Spirit, for it is your will that there be no famine of food or faith in the land, and that all should be fed.

For everything there is a time and a season. Regardless of the time or the season, you are still God, and we are still thankful. Amen.   —*Brad Braxton*

---

4. Parker J. Palmer, *Let Your Life Speak: Listening for the Voice of Vocation* (San Francisco: Jossey-Bass, 2000), 109.

Corporate Prayers
of Confession

O God, Mother and Father to us all, who in love has made us and through love has kept us, and who by love would make us perfect; we humbly confess that we have not loved you with all our heart and soul and mind and strength, and that we have not loved one another as Christ has loved us. Our selfishness has hindered your life within us. We have not lived by faith. We have resisted your Spirit. We have neglected your inspirations. Forgive what we have been; help us amend what we are; and by your Spirit direct what we shall be; that you may come into the full glory of your creation, in us, and in all; as in Jesus Christ our Lord. Amen.

Lord, we believe in thee; help thou our unbelief.
Lord, we love thee; yet not with perfect hearts.
Lord, we long for thee; yet not with our full strength.
Lord, we trust in thee; yet not with our whole selves.
O Lord, our Christ, may we have thy mind and thy spirit.

Make us contrite that we might be renewed from our sinful selves into new men and new women, according to thy will and for the sake of thy glory. Amen.

Prodded by conscience and the action of thy Spirit in our hearts, we humble ourselves before thee, gracious God, to make confession of our sins.

In the week just past we have bullied others with our power; set our hearts inordinately on some material possession; left at a shallow level relationships we might have deepened had we cared; disciplined our children in anger; saturated our minds with the world's bad news; and neglected the good news in which our faith is grounded.

Let our remembrance of these and other failings be accompanied in our minds by a saving remembrance of thy mercy. If thou, O God, shouldst mark iniquities, who of us could stand? We pray through Jesus Christ our Lord. Amen.

O thou who art the Giver of life, we confess how many times we have scorned thy gift. We find our hearts burdened with the memory of days refused or despised because we did not understand the opportunities that lay in them.

We confess before thee our many refusals to walk in thy way: vows we have made and forgotten, time we have frittered away, higher purposes in us we have allowed to grow weak. We confess all the goodness of life which we have received without giving thanks, all the beauties of this fair world which we have ignored, all the love coming to us from other human hearts which we have accepted carelessly.

O God, who art always more willing to give us more than we desire or deserve, come with forgiveness and healing to our confused lives and make us thine own. Through Jesus Christ our Lord. Amen.

Almighty and most merciful God, we come before thee in this season of bounty with our offering of confession. We acknowledge that we have heard the cry of the hungry and have turned silently away; we have heard the poor cry out for justice and have hardened our hearts.

Thou hast given us an earth of immeasurable riches, O God, and we have squandered its precious resources, only to pollute its waters and foul the very breath of life. We are quick to blame others, while we fail to see our own complicity in a world that predicates the bounty of few on the suffering of many.

Open our eyes, O God, and soften our hearts, that we may cheerfully do thy will to feed the hungry, clothe the naked, heal the sick. Bathe us in the healing waters of thy forgiveness, that we may start afresh and welcome each plea as a gift from thee, an opportunity to know thee in the sisters and brothers who call our name. In the name of Jesus Christ our Lord, who taught us to love by first loving us. Amen.

Almighty God, who didst bring again from the dead our Lord Jesus Christ, we acknowledge that we are unworthy of thy redeeming grace. We have not believed thy promises, for they are too good to believe, we being strangers to such goodness.

Blinded by our sorrows, we have not discerned Christ's presence with us. Through disappointment of mind and dejection of spirit, our hearts have not burned within us as we have heard his word. We have not believed in his redeeming power and have been overcome by evil. We have rejected the glad tidings of his victory over death, refusing to be comforted.

But now, in penitence, we come to thee, beseeching thy forgiveness. Mercifully grant us absolution from our sins, and restore unto us the joy of thy salvation. Amen.

In all truth, O God, and with much anguish, we confess that we have been poor stewards of thy good creation. We have sacrificed beauty on the altars of personal profit; upset the gentle balances of nature; commissioned the bulldozer to lay waste our legacy of unspoiled wilderness; and carelessly befouled the air we breathe.

Give us a due sense of the gravity of our mismanagement of life's resources; the promise of forgiveness; and the good sense so to temper our demands on nature, that we may work with thee and not against thee. Through Jesus Christ our Lord. Amen.

God of mercies, we acknowledge before thee our many sins and great shortcomings: how little we have denied ourselves for the sake of Christ; how much we have trusted in the wisdom of the world; how blind we have been to the true way of life; how deaf we have been to the call of thy word. O God, who art good and ready to forgive, change our wills that we may hate our sins with a perfect hatred and entirely forsake them. Bestow upon us thy merciful pardon; enable us to accept with meekness the remaining chastisement of the evil we have done; and grant that, our captivity being ended, we may freely serve thee in simple faith and humble love, all the rest of our life. Grant this for the sake of thy Son our Lord Jesus Christ. Amen.

O God, whose spirit keeps working in us and calling us to a loving community, we confess how often we have refused to acknowledge the wind of your Spirit blowing in our lives because we were not expecting it. We confess that we have been far more responsive to other winds: the winds of success and popularity, the winds of anxiety and despair, the winds of controversy and violence. We have often forgotten why we are and whose we are. It has seemed easier to extinguish a spark than to give ourselves to the transforming fire as the witnesses of a new order. Forgive us all that is past, and in this time of worship, help us find the courage to open ourselves in an act of awareness of the presence of the Spirit's wind in all of life. Amen.

Gracious God, behold us and hear us for the erring children that we are. Gifted with sight, we miss the glory that surrounds us; gifted with conscience, we make our peace with sin; gifted with the power to think, we fall for lies that cater to our prejudices; gifted with imagination, we plod along afraid to dream or hope; gifted with the quality of love, we waste our affection on things that matter little.

Forgive our gross misuse of life and grant that the very act of penitence itself may get us started in a new direction, lest we gain the world and lose our souls. Amen.

Eternal God, you make all things new and forgive old wrongs we can't forget. We confess we have spent time without loving and years without purpose, and the calendar condemns us. Daily we have done wrong and failed to do what you demand.

Forgive the past; do not let evil cripple or shame us. Lead us into the future, free from sin, free to love, and ready to work for your Son, our savior, Jesus Christ. Amen.

Forgive us, gracious God that we have allowed our worries to dominate our faith; that we are so swift to act and so slow to contemplate; that we know our world better than we know thy word; that we are selective with our indignation and uneven in expressing our compassion; that we harbor in our souls unspeakable jealousies and resentments; that our desire to be up-to-date has often put us out of touch with thee.

O thou whose mercy is ever greater than our sin, grant us thy pardon, and a true awareness of the same, to the end that here and now we may set out to serve thee in newness of life. Through Jesus Christ our Lord. Amen.

Eternal God, we confess our sins before thee, not to add to thy knowledge but to bring to our remembrance that which disturbs our communion with thee and limits our usefulness in thy service.

We have been blind to those faults in ourselves that we so easily detect in others: pleading the mystery of life even when the path of duty is clearly marked; reflecting the prejudices of the age rather than the mind of Christ; laboring and spending for that which does not satisfy; succumbing meekly to those who massage our wants and tell us what we need; easing up on self-control and calling it progress.

Give us, O God, one of thy choicest gifts, a sense of sin, and lead us from confession to penitence and pardon. Through Jesus Christ our Lord. Amen.

O God, whom we have come to know and love, hear us now for the erring children we know ourselves to be. We have honored thee with our lips, but our lives have not adorned the gospel.

We are too much like the age that environs us—coarse, violent, distraught, and frenzied. Too easily we have allowed our minds to be numbed by television, our hearts to be hardened against our neighbor's needs, our wills to be overrun by a fierce desire for acceptance. We have wasted thy gifts, misdirected our enthusiasms, neglected our faith, and fallen short of our potential.

Ashamed of these and all our sins, we humbly ask to be forgiven and restored. Through Jesus Christ our Lord. Amen.

God of our spirit, to whom our hearts lie open, hear thy people as in honesty and faith we make confession of our sin. With our tongues we have cut to shreds our neighbor's reputation. In our hearts we have despised those who did us wrong. Our minds have been the breeding ground of such fears and fantasies as betray a lack of trust in thee.

Careless in our worship, we have idolized at times family, race, and nation. Taken with our own importance, we have judged the rest of humankind by their resemblance to us. That we have no time for thee we take as much for granted as that thou shouldst have time for us.

From these and all our devious ways and doings, O God, deliver us, and let us to know thy pardon. Through Jesus Christ our Lord. Amen.

Ruler of all that is and is to be, sensitize our sight that we may see what really is and understand what ought to be. We confess that often we see only what we want to see. We complain about our vacations when thousands are cold and poverty-stricken. We speak of equal rights and justice for all but do not share the struggle for overcoming prejudices of race or nationality. We create technology but fail to control it. We enjoy the company of lively people but don't reach their loneliness.

You have given us life, O God, but we have not lived. You have called us to sing your song, but we have sung the message of the world instead. But here and now we admit our willfulness, we acknowledge our denial of your love, and we ask your forgiveness. Through Jesus Christ our Lord. Amen.

O loving Spirit, creator and sustainer of our lives, we admit in the only way we know how that we have fallen short of your plans for us. Forgetting that you have made us from your love, we have tried to stop loving ourselves and our neighbors. Forgetting that you have written your law upon our hearts, we have tried to stop thinking with the mind of Christ. Forgetting that your Spirit is sustaining us, we have tried to resist your guidance in the promptings of our souls.

We are weary of our own actions. Help us to know in heart, mind, and soul that you have forgiven us and are ready to lead us in your way everlasting. Through Jesus Christ our Lord. Amen.

Deliver us, O God, from the habit of blaming others for our faults and help us instead to become fluent in the language of confession. We acknowledge before thee our frequent lapses into sin; our failure to follow through on good intentions; the mediocrity of our faith; the devices we have developed to keep at a distance needs that we could have met; our tendency to label others according to our prejudices; our fear of the new; and our unwillingness to change.

Be patient with us yet awhile, and lead us, through penitence and trust, so to mend our ways, that we may more nearly resemble him whom we are pleased to call Master, Lord, and Friend. Amen.

O God, it isn't just the mistakes we've made again, nor the sores we have reopened and salted; it isn't only the week's new resentments, the new crop of grudges we've raised from the decay of dead dreams. These are only symptoms of what is really wrong. We are tired of patchwork. Our resolutions mock us: our promises expose us; our intentions depress us; our reforms ridicule us. We try to be whole apart from the Whole. We try to be real apart from the Real. You know what to do for us. In Jesus Christ our Lord. Amen.

O thou who hast made us for joy and not for sorrow, forgive us that the cities we build are so heavily marked by fear and death. Behind bolted doors we sit, neither seeking our neighbor's good nor finding our own. We look but do not see. We hear but do not listen. We crowd but do not touch. We reach but do not feel.

Forgive us our sins, O God. Lengthen our reach. Broaden our sympathies. And help us, as Jesus loved Jerusalem, to love this city that we call our home. In his strong name we pray. Amen.

Judge Eternal, God of love, we confess we have not made of peace a cause to fight and win for all your people. We have fed hungry missiles, not hungry mouths. We have squandered precious resources for immediate death instead of conserving them for future lives. We have prayed for peace, but we have not worked for peace with half the passion of those who plan for war. O God of mercy, forgive our great indifference and our little faith.

We come to you for forgiveness for the past and for strength to take another step for peace in the future. Amen.

Merciful God, we open ourselves before thee to acknowledge that we do not represent thy kingdom well. We suffer from failures of nerve, dimness of vision, divided allegiances, withheld compassion, wasted time, and intemperate speech. Minor irritations and petty satisfactions have closed us off against the good, the beautiful, and the true. It is scarcely clear to us, much less to others, that we intend to follow Jesus.

Cleanse us of these and all our sins and faults. Bless us with the gift of a fresh start and a new resolve. And all to the end that our frail but forgiven lives may winsomely declare thy praise. Through Jesus Christ our Lord. Amen.

O God, who loves us in so many ways, we confess that we have not lived up to your expectations. Even when we have tried our best, we seem to lose control. We thank you for being so patient and so understanding as to put up with our unfaithfulness. You have asked us to be loving and kind, and instead we have turned away from one another. You have tried to teach us to love in peace, and instead we have been constantly in conflict, even with those who love us most. We have been selfish and careless in the things we do, when we should have been thoughtful and caring.

Forgive us, O God, for acting this way, and help us learn to be the people we were meant to be. Help us to respect others, to be honest with ourselves, and to be forgiving because we know you have forgiven us. We ask this in the name of your Son, Jesus Christ. Amen.

O God, eternal source of wisdom, power, and love, we confess the superficiality of our lives. We live in the midst of haste and confusion without the wisdom to renew ourselves by quiet and withdrawal. We listen to the voices that whisper to us of ease and caution and compromise when we should be listening to your Spirit. We have deceived ourselves by thinking that perpetual movement is action.

Forgive us, O God. Lift our vision, that we may see how frantic our lives really are. Make us feel the compulsion of your indwelling love and the confidence that comes from dwelling in it. Through Jesus Christ our Lord. Amen.

O thou who art both merciful and just, we accept thy gracious invitation to confess. By our own standards we have fallen short. How much more have we sinned against thy holy law! Forgive us our fear of the new, our presumptions of righteousness, the stinginess of our love, and our preference for convenience in religion rather than conviction.

Where we are truly sorry for our sins, let us hear the word of pardon and receive the benediction of thy peace. Amen.

A City-Dweller's Prayer

O God of every time and place,
  prevail among us too;
within the city that we love
  its promise to renew.
Our people move with downcast eyes,
  tight, sullen, and afraid.
Surprise us with thy joy divine,
  for we would be remade.

O thou whose will we can resist,
  but cannot overcome,
forgive our harsh and strident ways,
  the harm that we have done.
Like Babel's builders long ago
  we raise our lofty towers,
and like them too our words divide,
  and pride lays waste our powers.

Behind the masks that we maintain
  to shut our sadness in,
there lurks the hope, however dim,
  to live once more as kin.
Let wrong embolden us to fight
  and need excite our care;
If not us, who? If not now, when?
  If not here, God, then where?

Our forebears stayed their minds on thee
    in village, farm, and plain.
Help us, their crowded, harried kin,
    no less thy peace to claim.
Give us to know that thou dost love
    each soul that thou hast made,
that size does not diminish grace,
    nor concrete hide thy gaze.

Grant us, O God, who labor here
    within this throbbing maze
a forward-looking, saving hope
    to galvanize our days.
Let Christ, who loved Jerusalem,
    and wept its sins to mourn,
make just our laws and pure our hearts;
    so shall we be reborn! Amen.

—Ernest T. Campbell